Jack the Rip

In my blood

Norman Kirtlan and Dianne Bainbridge

Published by Stone Boy Books

C184863860

First published in 2013

2nd edition April 2014

Copyright: Norman Kirtlan

ISBN:

978-0-9926979-0-7

Published by

Stone Boy Books,

Washington

stoneboybooks@gmail.com

JACK the RIPPER

In my blood

Who will you find? The tantalising question posed by a genealogy company encourages us to dig deep into their archives in the hope of finding those long lost ancestors. Indeed that journey can be both fascinating and rewarding, turning up paupers and princes and a few other surprises along the way.

But, when that journey takes you back to a time and a place and a person whose very name strikes fear into the hearts of a nation, then you may well take a deep breath and wonder if it is in your best interests to journey further, but of course you will ignore your doubts and carry on.

When your journey takes you back to the streets of Whitechapel, and when the year is 1888 and there is only one name on everyone's lips – you will try very hard to drag your ancestor back into line; to become anonymous; to be an innocent watcher in the crowd.

But when your ancestor will not let you escape – what will you do then?

Cold Case

It is very easy to present chapter upon chapter of wholly circumstantial evidence, thereafter offering your candidate as the one and only Ripper; it is very easy to announce to the world that you have "closed the case", charging Walter Sickert or Aaron Kosminski or some hitherto unheard-of chap in New Zealand with multiple murders. It is very easy, but also very foolish.

The simple fact exists that although no one will ever be brought to book for the brutal slaying of Annie Chapman and her unfortunate friends, if one proffers a suspect, albeit one hundred and twenty five years after the event, then one needs sufficient evidence to satisfy judge and jury of guilt. There needs to be more than a physical deformity that *may* have resulted in a hatred of women, or the finding of a ticket from the Whitechapel Road Pawn Shop dated August 1888 which *may* have put our chap and his victim in the same street in the same month. The laws of libel do not apply to the dead, but we must always bear in mind that the dead do not have a right to respond to the mischief of the living.

To satisfy a court of law, one needs overwhelming evidence. Even confessions alone will not these days suffice. We need DNA; photographs, physical evidence that puts our man at the scene; corroborated witness reports and a multitude of other, tangible ingredients that will, together, convince our jury of guilt.

Needless to say, this book does not seek to close the case. This book does not crassly name he or she who is undoubtedly the Whitechapel murderer, thereby spurning every other suspect who has or who will be put forward for these most horrific crimes. Instead this book soberly tells the story of one woman's journey. It tells of a chance discovery; a conundrum that, when unlocked, led directly to Whitechapel. It tells of the piecing together of a jigsaw that asked more questions than it answered.

We look at the extraordinary evidence that our traveller-in-time uncovered in the exploration of her ancestor's world: His journeys, his crimes, the inexplicable covering up of his footsteps.

We take our man away from London and on to the North East of England. He is there when more murders are committed. He is caught and brought to book for just one of his crimes. His deeds, his cover ups and his attempt to remain anonymous have remained, just as he desired, slumbering and forgotten for over a century. But there was one thing that he overlooked: a simple piece of paper; a tiny and perplexing clue that would awaken him and his world and offer him forward as yet another candidate for the Whitechapel Murders.

Interwoven with the story of our ancestor, we revisit the infamous murders and chronicle the events that made this period of time such a dark stain upon our history. We explore the profile and the background; we look at the flaws in contemporary police evidence and the miscarriage of justice that let the killer carry on his work, and thereafter sleep, safe in the knowledge that in death, his crimes – and his identity – would be buried along with his reposing corpse.

Until now, that is...

A closed mind is a dead mind.

The first murder scene that I attended was back in the spring of 1975; I had no more than a walk-on part, standing guard, shooing away curious onlookers and maintaining a log that recorded the attendance of those with something more to contribute than I: senior detectives, the forensic pathologist, and latterly they who would carefully remove the body to the mortuary prior to a post mortem examination.

Part of my role was to lead the eminent professionals from the front door of the terraced council house, through a predetermined *safe route* and up into the actual scene of the crime – a small double bedroom at the back of the dwelling. And even though my hands would not be bloodied by the meticulous piecing together and collection of evidence that would take place that day, the experience of sharing that small place with the industry of murder – and indeed the corpse itself – would be an incredibly moving event for me.

The victim lay on his back on a mattress that was already saturated in blood; his head, or what was left of it, had been battered by a claw hammer and pieces of bone and brain were stuck to the head of the weapon, which lay on the pillow beside him, just as the murderer had left it. The whole scene was watched over by walls that resembled the paintings of Jackson Pollock – an overlay of steadily browning spatter that all but covered the peeling flowered wallpaper beneath.

It was difficult to see the victim's eyes as they were veiled by matted hair and the debris left behind after his killing, but closer inspection revealed that they were half open, peering out into the room, witness to events that were unfolding for his benefit and following his tragic demise.

There is something about the smell of death that touches all who breathe it; there is something about the cocktail of odours that emanate from a scene of great violence that, once tasted will never be forgotten. This was my first experience of its like, and my face must have reflected a circus of feelings that were bubbling below the surface. An arm on my shoulder woke me from those dark machinations.

The old detective who stood before me clutching a bag full of exhibits and grinning in recognition of my symptoms, nodded towards the corpse and offered words of advice that have stayed with me over the years. "The key to survival is very simple," he said. "Don't get involved, son. Detach yourself. If you don't, then you will end up as much a victim as our friend on the bed there!"

I knew exactly what he was talking about and he was one hundred percent correct. What I was seeing and experiencing for the first time that day was a psychological ouch! A wakening of senses that had to be controlled. There was no doubt that I could have walked away from that room and chalked it up as just another job experience; something that had to be done without question – death, after all was as much a part of the career that I had signed up to as was directing traffic and looking for lost children. But when the corpse becomes someone's father, someone's son – and that *someone* is dying of a broken heart because you just knocked at their front door in your pointy helmet and gave out the bad news – well that's the point where you have to take a deep breath and step outside of your emotions. Don't get involved - see the job with an open mind; for only then will what lies before you be washed by clarity. It was a lesson that I learned well during my thirty one years as a police officer and a lesson that I still use to this day. It was also something that flashed across my mind in November 2012 when I took the telephone call from Dianne Bainbridge. "Can you spare me a few minutes?" the voice was quiet and somewhat apprehensive, but I sensed strength behind it.

"Yes, of course."

"You'll probably think I'm mad..."

Well, I didn't think that she was mad, but then again I had taken my usual step back. I was listening and seeing and thinking without judgement or emotion. This was indeed another first. No one had ever confided in me that an ancestor may have been linked to the Whitechapel murders of 1888. I suppose, in retrospect, nobody would have blamed me if I had asked more questions or posed a test or two to measure the sanity of my caller, but there was one ingredient more than any other that convinced me that this tale was worthy of further investigation. Dianne was not "closing the case", far from it. She was trying hard to take her ancestor away from Flower and Dean Street and Mitre Square – not force him down a path that would squeeze him into a dangerous conviction – as has happened in so many miscarriages of justice over the years.

Dianne simply wanted a second opinion. Should she carry on digging or should she abandon her ancestor to the mysterious circumstances wherein he had been discovered some months before? It was entirely her decision, but I felt that if she were to close the book on her unnamed chap (she had at this stage kept his identity close to her chest) – then she would spend the rest of her days wondering. No, even with the scant pieces of the jigsaw that she had given me, it was obvious that she had to carry on and of course I offered to help her in her endeavours.

In order that she could assess my own opinion and thoughts relating to Jack the Ripper and his alleged crimes, and thereby supplement her own knowledge of that dark place in which her ancestor had found himself, I suggested that she attend a talk that I was giving the next week on the subject of the Ripper, his crimes and his profile.

At the end of that night and following subsequent discussions, two appetites were very much whetted. It was time to throw my own investigative experience into the ring. It was also time to get to know the lady whose endeavours had brought about our meeting and who was about to open the book on her work thus far.

Dianne Bainbridge is a businesswoman; she is a gritty Northerner possessed of all the right ingredients for success: She is clear thinking and determined; she does not suffer fools gladly and she questions before accepting information that presents itself. When conundrums come her way she attacks them with the same vigour that she applies to her commercial endeavours.

It was hardly surprising that when some years ago, Dianne set about searching for her birth parents, as many adoptees do, that she would apply the same logic and determination to the task that lay ahead. It was a journey that would not only prove to be both fruitful and rewarding, but it would also highlight genealogy as an enjoyable pastime. It would be a skill that would be put to very good use shortly afterwards, when a relative handed her a small Memento Mori card, wondering if it were worthy of further investigation.

The card had long puzzled its owners, the Williams family, who had owned it for as long as anyone could remember. It was one of those little mysteries that sit in a tin box alongside photographs and souvenirs and all of the flotsam that passes down from one generation to the next.

Dianne accepted the challenge and examined the first piece of a puzzle that would consume her time and passion for years to come. But, for now, holding this tiny scrap of age-worn card, it seemed that the only destination that the initial clue would lead was straight down a blind alley.

James Walter Robert Webber. Who on earth was James Walter Robert Webber? The family who owned the card were the Williams, so no link there. The Webber surname did evoke a distant memory, but the family concerned were Devonians and the card made reference to a small church at East Finchley in London: All very confusing - but, times dates and places are all important ingredients in the genealogist's journey and, at least, this was a start.

Holy Trinity Church in East Finchley is a squat sandstone building that sits huddled behind tall yew trees and a hedge of evergreen holly. Its bell tower is modest to say the least, and one could drive through the suburban landscape that surrounds it, never noticing the church or the great and the good who rest in its graveyard.

But, for all its modesty and quiet seclusion, Holy Trinity provided Dianne with a stepping stone into the past. It was the place where the grandly named James Walter Robert Webber could be placed for a few hours in time; the place where he said goodbye to this world and was welcomed by the next.

Memento Mori and Yet More Questions.

Say what you like about the Victorians, but they loved a good death; the poor souls saw enough of it and in the words of a contemporary observer, they were damned good at it!   The passing of a loved one was a social occasion and one that demanded strict adherence to the dark rules of etiquette. Clocks were stopped, mirrors covered, curtains drawn and lengths of crepe were hung sombrely on doorknockers and handles: black for an adult and white for a child. James Webber would, if his parents were so minded, have adorned their brasses in pure white, for he was only seven years of age when he departed this life in the early spring of 1888.

JAMES WALTER ROBERT WEBBER

BORN 11TH DECEMBER 1881

DIED 7TH MARCH 1888

INTERNMENT 10TH MARCH 1888

HOLY TRINITY CHURCH, EAST FINCHLEY.

During the second week of March that year, his father would have handed over a few shillings to the local printer and secured for himself a box containing a hundred or so Memento Mori cards, each the size of a modern credit card, and each bearing the pertinent details of his dead son.

As friends and relations came to pay their last respects and examine the mortal remains of young James, they would have been handed a card as both remembrance and souvenir. Those who came to the funeral on 10th March would likewise take away a card from a pile at the back of the church. One of those tiny cards had been treasured enough to have been kept and passed down through three or more generations; but by whom and why? The questions were mounting. Answers were still a long way off.

Who were the Webber family? This was the first question that Dianne had to answer. The name just didn't have any relevance to her relations and ancestors and every check that Dianne carried out showed that the name had no obvious significance; and East Finchley! Bearing in mind that the little card was discovered by family in Hartlepool and again there was no known link to London – it seemed that the best thing to do would be to abandon the search there and then. It was probably someone else's family – an anonymous little curio that someone had pushed out of sight and forgotten about for over a century and surely not be worth the effort of further enquiry.

But Dianne Bainbridge doesn't give up that easily. Someone had thought this child important enough to hang on to his Memento Mori; someone had been touched by sorrow at James' passing and had kept this little treasure as a heartfelt remembrance. No, there would be no giving up on little James Webber. Whoever he was, Dianne was determined to find out. Perhaps it was her maternal instinct switching on and taking over when she announced, "This child deserved to belong to someone. He had lived and died on this scrap of paper, but I was giving him his identity back. No one else would do this, and if this card were to be lost then he would slip into obscurity forever." The computer was switched on and enquiries began in earnest.

Every ten years, commencing in 1841, a census of the population was carried out by an army of pencil and ledger wielding clerks who knocked on doors up and down the country, gathering information vital to the governments of the day. Who lived here? Who was head of the house? Occupations, places of birth and the odd spurious comment were often thrown in by footsore and grumpy old enumerators. If ever there was a document that would unravel the past and provide a complete snapshot in time, then the census record was it. But, once again, nothing would come easily in the identification of young James.

Born just months after the 1881 census, and dying three years prior to the next, in May 1891, the lad would never be recorded. Regardless of how many Webbers there were in East Finchley, putting the right family to our particular youngster was beyond the official census. Young James was proving just as mischievous a lad in death as he probably was in life. Dianne was starting to feel a strange affinity to the lad and the more she pondered upon her young charge, the more she was determined to give him his proper place in history. Perhaps his death certificate – if indeed one existed - would hold a clue and take her search to the next level.

When the postman eventually delivered an official envelope to her door, Dianne could finally add more names, facts and a speculative picture or two to the mystery. Young James was no longer an orphan in time; his father, William John Webber now sprang to life. The two were reunited once more on an embryonic family tree. In addition, a third family member was named on the certificate. She who had been present as young James had struggled through chronic respiratory infection and painfully breathed his last: Annie Jenkins Belcher, James' older, married sister.

With a little more research, the tree began to spread its branches even further. Belcher – a new name and more chances to make sense of the connections twixt north and south. Soon, with the arrival of Annie Jenkins' marriage certificate Dianne was introduced to someone new: William Benjamin Belcher. The name would later come back to haunt her, but at this stage that is all he was – a ghost from the past. Putting flesh onto the skeleton would take time, as William Belcher was not going to give up his secrets without a long hard struggle.

More names, more avenues to explore. The introduction of a new surname meant that Dianne could extend her family tree of three and forge on into the future; problem was, the future, like the family's past, was beginning to get a little bit complicated, particularly when Dianne tried to take the Belcher family beyond the year 1888. William Benjamin and his brood seemed to disappear into thin air - all very strange indeed.

The years prior to 1888 were a little easier to research, and soon Dianne could paint a better picture of the coming together of those families who would play a significant part in the lives of William Belcher and his wife Annie Jenkins Webber, neither of whom would be blessed with pedigrees of great distinction.

Nature or nurture?

It is an argument that will always provide fodder for those who struggle with its relevance to the lives of good and bad and all who lie between. Are killers brewed in the womb or do they learn their trade at the hands of their elders and betters? Many will tell us that those with a penchant for evil have an unstable parentage; absent fathers and overbearing mothers. Would Josef Fritzl have been a better father if his mother hadn't swung between beating him skinless and protecting him from the nasty old world outside? Would Jerry Brudos have found torture, slavery and murder so tasteful if his mother hadn't preferred a daughter to the gangling son that she bore? If she had let the bairn get over his fascination with ladies' high heeled shoes without whipping him raw, would he still have cut off a woman's leg to model his favourite stiletto heels?

Perhaps we will never know the answer to these questions, and unfortunately for those who delve into the minds of our dysfunctional Victorian ancestors, the records simply do not exist that will give us that degree of insight into their early years. Those we glean are lean indeed, and putting fat onto old bones is difficult to say the least. Skeletons in the cupboards of the Belcher family would show enough though, to give Dianne a flavour of William

Benjamin's early years, and perhaps reason or two for what would later transpire.

Benjamin Belcher, William's father, was born in Chelsea in 1843. His travels, always within the capital, weaved a trail that would drop stitches here and there and even confuse the census enumerators, who would pencil in his name and then strike him off as an afterthought. He can be traced from Chelsea to St Marylebone, where as a locksmith he married his sweetheart Ellen Percy, in 1863. His trade then changes to house painter, before he disappears again and turns up in Grove Street, Marylebone, in 1891.

His wife Ellen was also a Londoner. In 1867, while Benjamin was on his travels, she earned herself six months imprisonment for thievery. By 1880 she had died, to be replaced by a matriarchal aunt who was drafted in to care for the young family. In 1888, with Benjamin still some years from making his prodigal return, the Belchers were right in the thick of the fun and games that were rocking Whitechapel – and the rest of Victorian Society. Leaning out from the windows of their terraced rooms in Grove Street, the Belchers, and the lodger with whom the new Mrs B. had set up home, could not fail to feel the almost tangible fear as Ripper fever gripped the streets around her.

Ellen's son William Benjamin Belcher, already established with his young family at 20 Grove Street was for reasons best known to himself, spending 1888 travelling between London and the North East of England. When back in the capital he was gainfully employed at a Dairy Supply Company in Dorset Street, a business that had learned well from the plagues of the past and which was, thanks to the new methods of pasteurisation, a thriving concern.

Carrying great churns of milk for ten hours a day would have probably endowed young William with a powerful physique - and as any wrestler will tell you, such exercise would build those muscles particularly associated with a grip that could help lock his arms immovably around any potential victim – should he be so inclined, of course.

His work would also place him on the streets during those same pre dawn hours favoured by the Whitechapel murderer. But these details were as yet unknown to Dianne, who was still simply adding flesh to her burgeoning family tree. It would take one more good hard look at the details that she had thus far ascertained before the first uneasy feelings settled upon this little adventure of hers. Laid out before her was the great family tree. And a few questions were begging immediate answers.

The first mystery was that "other" family up north. She knew that William was constantly up and down on the Great North Eastern Railway, but what for? Perhaps he was visiting the Williams family whom she knew formed the earliest ancestors of her Hartlepool family. But the more she looked at the Hartlepool folks, the more that something jumped out and demanded further investigation. The first unfortunate coincidence.

(Hartlepool) William Williams. Born Paddington 1864. (Whitechapel) William Benjamin Belcher, born Paddington 1864.

(Hartlepool) Annie Williams, born Budleigh Salterton 1862. (Whitechapel) Annie Jenkins Webber, born Budleigh Salterton 1862. (See appendix 2 and 3)

The Hartlepool family had a daughter, whose name was Kate Ellen Williams. The census told Dianne that she had been born in Paddington in 1886. Further delving into the records showed that the Belchers down south also had a daughter. Surprise, surprise: Kate Ellen Belcher, born Paddington 1886

At this point Dianne was left scratching her head. What on earth was going on? This whole episode just did not make sense. Yes, of course, it was now obvious that the two "families" were one and the same. When later searches revealed 1888 to be the year that William Benjamin Belcher and his little brood simply fell off the census records - stopped existing according to Dianne, that's when the stomach sinks and you want to put this whole mystery into the same tin box that contained the memento mori card and let it go back to sleep for another hundred years or so.

Together with very helpful staff at the Hartlepool Library, Dianne trawled all of the records to see if the Williams featured there prior to 1888. They didn't. She trawled the London records to see if her Belchers tarried beyond 1888. They didn't. It was obvious that the Belchers had, in a very short time, simply morphed into the Williams'.

So what the hell was William – whatever his name was – playing at? What was going on in Whitechapel that would necessitate a quick and very comprehensive getaway? Surely Victorian London wasn't that bad?

It was only when she decided to trawl the internet in an attempt to find out some background information on the place where William and his young family had once lived – and had hastily left, that the penny finally dropped.

Whitechapel 1888 – it seemed like an innocuous enough search. Perhaps, she thought, naively, there may be the odd description of the streets, the social conditions and the background to mass exodus. What came back was Jack – and lots of it. Dianne had never considered the infamous murders, nor had she previously put two and two together. After all, this kind of thing just wasn't within the remit of her enquiry, nor was it the kind of subject that remotely interested her.

OK, so her chap was geographically very close to the nightmare that was the Ripper, but so were thousands of others. Funny thing is, when it's your own flesh and blood, you become protective; you want to get your lad safely away from all of that nonsense. But instead of becoming more and more anonymous, William Belcher seemed reluctant to let go of his roots. And what's more, a series of unfortunate coincidences and occurrences were waiting in the genealogical wings.

Being both a mother and an individual possessed of a moral conscience, Dianne's first thoughts turned to practical family matters. Why on earth had William Belcher, aka Williams, chosen to leave not just his home, but *his* dear old mother? After all, living just yards away from the epicentre of murder, it was hardly conducive with the old girl's safety, was it?

And yes, the lady was, by all accounts, a wily old devil, hardened by such things as her short stay in Wormwood Scrubs, but it still did not make sense. And perhaps all of this name change carry-on was just a family thing – after all, Mother had successfully changed her name from Ellen to Margaret. No, it still did not make sense. (Dianne would later realise that Margaret was another relation who had slipped into the void left by his mother's death and assumed the family name.)

Somewhere in all of that internet information about the Ripper, Dianne recalled a simple profile that had been suggested by a contemporary psychologist. Perhaps, she thought, if she applied this to her William, then some of those nagging doubts might go away. Out came the print out, out came the pencil; the object of the exercise being to put as much distance between her ancestor and foul deeds in the capital as she possibly could.

a) Circle hypothesis. Serial killers live within seven miles of first offence(s). Well, she certainly couldn't chalk the first one off. After all, Grove Street was in spitting distance of Jack's territory.
b) He would be male. Second one conceded.
c) He would be 25 to 35 years of age. Bingo.
d) No father figure. Yep, Benjamin was hardly the stay-at-home type.
e) A familiar person, known locally to all and sundry. OK. The local milkman might be a familiar personage, despite his nocturnal ramblings.

f) He may have possessed police knowledge. Dianne's initial smugness at pencilling a line through this could have been rather premature, for reasons that we will later discuss.

g) He would have anatomical knowledge – more than likely through butchery. Our milkman may well have had triceps like an all in wrestler, but the internal workings of the female reproductive system didn't seem like a likely exam question for a job at the Dairy Supply Company. Another pencil line and back to the books. Time to look at the in-laws.

Budleigh Salteron, Butchers and Bankruptcy

Budleigh Salterton is the kind of place that the travelling Victorian only came upon by accident. Separated from Exmouth, its grander neighbour, by a swathe of green fields, Budleigh Salterton probably slept on while the Industrial Revolution was grinding out smoke, sparks and fumes in those busier places up north.

Pebble beaches roll gently down to the Channel while fishing boats slumber in the Devon sunshine. The town it seems was never one to attract attention to itself; the dwellings along the bay nestled quietly and unobtrusively in their hollow; a sleeping jewel in the vast Jurassic coast and also home to William John Webber.

If Budleigh Salterton was content in its anonymity, proud of its peaceful solitude, then William John Webber was going to change all that. Born in 1841, William was the original party animal. Drink and tobacco fuelled fists that were rarely hidden from sight, and William, already destined for a life in the family firm, would take to business like a duck to water. The ingredients for a life dealing in death were already in place. A sharp knife, a strong grip and the stomach to slice open a throat and bathe in warm blood while one's victim struggled out its last moments on this earth. And once the object of his endeavours hung quietly on the steel hook above him, young William would soon acquire the knowledge required to slice open a carcass and carefully explore that which lay within. All very necessary skills for a butcher in Budleigh Salterton.

On 26th February 1862, young William, according to the Western Times, was hosting a riotous party within the salubrious surroundings of a yard at the back of the butchery business, when, quite literally, all hell broke loose. Of the dozens of drunken teenagers who were present, two were very much in love with a lusty young shoe binder named Sarah Smith. In order that they might decide which of the two had conjugal rights over the girl, they set about each other in a contest to determine superiority.

William Webber, with threats aplenty, decided to turn out the rioters, and using such promises as knocking blocks off and stabbing the participants with a knife, set about the ejections. Sarah Smith objected vociferously to these actions, whereupon, according to witnesses she was unceremoniously booted into the arms of her brother. Sarah responded by slapping William about the face.

In appeasement William duly offered the use of his yard for a private contest between the two suitors, a bout that was to take place at a later time, but Sarah Smith's womenfolk had already been summoned by one of the lads present and a posse of impending violence was clattering through the cobbled streets heading for "Greedy's Yard".

In the melee that followed, Webber would go head to head in a few rounds of what one witness described as "cat clawing" with George Horn Hooper. As is often the case with such incidents - and in particular when the witnesses are each as drunk as the other, the resulting court case would collapse into mayhem, the magistrates dismissing the lot with a stern warning and moans aplenty about "the youth of today".

At the time of the incident, William Webber was already a married man, having promised his future to Catherine Jenkins just a few months previous. It was a future that held little in the way of joy for Catherine, as her husband's wild nature would repeatedly come to the fore, and she would find herself an unwilling victim to his bouts of violence.

On New Year's Day 1870, William, fuelled by drink, exploded into violence and struck his young wife, sending her sprawling across the floor. While he slept off his anger, Catherine fled from the house and sought refuge with her parents. It wasn't the done thing to complain about domestic violence in those dark days, as women were very much chattels for men to do with them what they would, but Catherine, encouraged by her mother, found herself hammering on the door of local bobby, Police Constable Adams.

The officer invited the woman inside, examined her injuries and listened carefully to her story. When asked if she was prepared to make a statement and take her husband to court, Catherine said that she was. Out came the pencil and Catherine Webber scratched her name to the allegation of malicious assault. Constable Adams slipped the evidence into his tunic pocket and went out in search of his suspect.

The Feather's Commercial Inn down at the Budleigh Salterton High Street was heaving with customers when the officer pushed open the doors and peered through the smoke, looking for William John Webber. He was there of course, propping up the bar and already well oiled. The officer invited Webber out into the street and showed him the warrant charging him with assault. Webber shrugged his shoulders and went along to the lock up without a fuss, but with that old fire burning away within his stomach. No sooner had the policeman opened the cell doors and reached over to search his prisoner – something that a wiser old copper should have done back on the High Street, than William Webber reached into his pockets and pulled out a spring loaded knife, slashing out at his captor.

The officer backed off sharply, but in holding up his hand to fend off the blow, Webber's knife sliced into his finger. Bloodied and shocked, Police Constable Adams fought back and overpowered the hefty young butcher, throwing him into the cells until he sobered up enough to be charged.

At Exeter Assizes, Webber would claim that because the knife was so stiff, he left it in the open position to save effort next time he used it. Preferring to believe that his was nothing more than the tool of any common thug, the court found him guilty of assaulting the policeman. William John Webber was dragged off to begin a three month sentence of imprisonment. His wife and three young daughters, Annie, Sarah and Charlotte would fall on the mercy of the parish in order to survive.

That the family business was destined to fail is little wonder. With William at its head, the hard drinking, hard hitting butcher obviously found hedonistic activities more enjoyable than hard graft. In July 1876, he was declared bankrupt and with yet another to add to the brood, he and Catherine (already pregnant with daughter number five) upped sticks and sought a living in Bedford.

After a brief spell as an Industrial Assurance Agent, William packed his bags once more and headed for the capital. By 1881, he was once again slitting the throats of those creatures great and small as a butcher in East Finchley.

It was there that the Webbers and the Belchers came together. William Benjamin Belcher met and fell in love with Annie, the Webber's oldest daughter. The mad butcher now had a prospective son in law as an apprentice and the circle of life was complete.

For Dianne Bainbridge, the coming together of her ancestors was another lead weight in her stomach. By the beginning of 1888, her man had ticked off another of those criterion required by every good serial killer, and in particular the one from Whitechapel. Our nocturnal milkman had skills beyond the churn: he could slit a bloody good throat too.

Dianne of course was still comparing her chap's profile against the naive shortlist that she had uncovered in an internet search. We will look much more deeply in the next few chapters at the profiling of our murderer, but what, I joked, of the unticked box on her list? Are there any police connections here? Does William Belcher have knowledge of police procedure – sufficient to be able to predict movements and modus operandi?

Dianne opens up her family tree and points at William Belcher's brother, Charles. By 1892 she tells me, there is a detective sergeant by the same name in the Metropolitan Police. At the time of the murders, he is learning his trade on the streets of the East End. (Should this individual and Belcher's brother not be same person, there is indeed another related police office by the name of Barrett, whom we shall mention later.) The coincidences kept on coming, but I needed more. I needed something that would give me a flavour of this man's personality. All too often this is the ingredient that one finds impossible to determine in those family tree searches. Names and occupations are one thing, but how about something that would give me an insight into the inner workings of William Benjamin Belcher?

Dianne believes that she can give me that too. In 1886, on his travels up and down to the North East, William, under his alias William Williams, is sentenced to six months imprisonment for raping a girl aged between 13 and 16. An interesting development indeed, but one that needs to be fine tuned when records are available.

A decade previous to this offence, the age of consent for females was raised from twelve to thirteen years. Unthinkable these days, but at a time when the most important thing was the reputation of the "gentleman", girls were strictly second class citizens. Following an unethical undercover newspaper investigation into child prostitution, during which William Thomas Stead *bought* a thirteen year old girl, Eliza Armstrong, ostensibly for a night of sex, things would change. (Coincidentally, this all occurred in the next street to the Belcher's London home.)

Stead took the girl to a local midwife in order that she might be proven to be a virgin. Today this kind of behaviour would be deemed an horrific assault on the child's dignity and person.

Armstrong was then taken to a brothel, and readers of the newspaper were led to believe that she was drugged and raped. Such was the outcry among the gentlefolk of Britain that the law was changed before the week was out. In 1875, a girl could not give consent until she had reached sixteen years of age. A special offence was created to cover the dubious area twixt thirteen and sixteen, which in effect, watered down the severity and punishment associated with what was still the rape of young teens.

This offence, if it can be attributed to our William, was significant for another reason too. While many purists will argue that a penchant for young teenagers does not equate to the later murder of mature prostitutes and that serial killers do not change, we all know that this is just not true. The effect that capture, stigmatisation and imprisonment has on a man who is driven by and sees his future in sexual offences is often demonstrated in a complete change of modus operandi. (M.O) Rapists will murder their victims to stop them from talking. Victims will be selected from different groups and different places, knowing full well that the risk is reduced by careful selection. Disorganised offenders learn from the experience and plan a little more carefully.

Consider too, hedonistic lust killers like Dennis Rader whose victims ranged from nine years of age to sixty two. For men like him, it is not the victim that is important but the act, and more particularly, the process; the fear in his subject and the excitement that he derives from her terror. Thus we cannot yet eliminate our William from future terror and the murder of older women.

In short, while the jury was very much still in deliberation over William Benjamin Belcher, there were enough points of relevance and interest to allow his tenure as a credible suspect to exist a little longer.

There were more remarkable discoveries yet to come, but for the time being we will leave our candidate where he stands and try to answer Dianne's question. In a rethink of the Whitechapel murders, would the police in 2013 be knocking at 20 Grove Street and asking William to pop down to the station for a little chat?

Those in 1888 would have had to act quickly, as by the end of November that year he, his pregnant wife and the rest of the family – including their lodger - had upped sticks, changed their name for good and were in hiding up in Hartlepool.

Ripperology and Behavioural Evidence Analysis.

I have to admit that the whole Ripperology thing sits uncomfortably in my mind, but that opinion is derived due to a band of unhealthy individuals who associate themselves with this enquiry. That someone would devote his or her entire life to a century old murder spree and he who perpetrated those crimes is, I find, an incredible commitment. But why just Jack? After all, we do not have diehard Fred Westologists or Hindleyologists – so why indeed the Ripper?

Perhaps my judgement is clouded by conversations and death threats – yes death threats – from one or two of their number. One nutter threatened to "tear out my uterus" in an anonymous and threatening letter after a talk that I presented locally. The police officer who informed me of the threat asked me if I wished to make a formal complaint about the matter. On the grounds that the author would have a hard job to find the aforementioned organ should he jump out on me in some dark alley, (and indeed I had a good idea who had sent the letter - I had seen him sitting drooling at the back of the hall on the night of the talk) I had little problem in asking the officer to drop the crudely scripted threat in the nearest bin.

Another chap who took exception to the thoughts that I presented, (some based on Karyo Magelan's masterful work, "By Ear and Eyes"), voiced his opinions in a distinctly disturbing and aggressive manner. Bearing the open minded maxim I adopted as my starting point, I asked the good fellow a few questions in order to gauge his ability and qualifications. If I was to cross swords with an expert it was important that I took up the correct defensive stance.

"How many murders have you investigated?"

"None."

"How many crime scenes have you attended?"

"None".

"Have you actually seen a dead body before?"

"I saw my Grandad..."

The chap was a taxi driver who had obviously read a Ripper book once; felt that the whole Jack the Ripper thing was incredibly sexy and decided to set himself up as a *Ripperologist*. I put down the telephone and wrote him off as another idiot.

That one or two individuals have set themselves a task of presenting for mass consumption, just about every known shred of evidence and circumstance relating to the murders is laudable, and I admire their sterling work. There is however a fine line betwixt science and voyeurism. The latter group, deriving vicarious pleasure and thrills from murders that have gone before, have no more place in literature – or society – than any other dangerous individual. That they tarnish the work of the serious enquirer and presenter of evidence is without doubt.

No self respecting authority on Jack the Ripper will close his or her book on any individual or preclude any other contemporary murder as being definitely not one of Jack's without very careful consideration – and indeed a lot more evidence than we could possibly garner a century after the event. Paul Begg's book, *Jack the Ripper, the facts,* is a wonderful example of such an authority: he brings to the table the known ingredients, together with a list of those suspects who have been thrown into the frame over the years. He writes with authority, and importantly for a work that demands respect, without the emotion associated with the uterus-ripper-outers.

And so, let us arm ourselves with the known facts, whether provided by Paul Begg or the internet site *casebook.org* or whomsoever we accept as a healthy source – and let us then join 1888 with 2013. If indeed we are going to measure the man, his crimes and his likely persona, then we have to combine the best of today's expertise with what remains of yesterday's crimes.

Dr. Thomas Bond, the registered police surgeon for A Division, Westminster, opened a brand new chapter in the investigation of serious crimes, when, following detailed studies of the Ripper victims, and in particular the murder of Mary Kelly, (whom Bond believed was killed by the same hand as Nichols, Chapman, Eddowes and Stride,) when he reported:

Assuming the murderer to be such a person as I have just described he would probably be solitary and eccentric in his habits, also he is most likely to be a man without regular occupation, but with some small income or pension. He is possibly living among respectable persons who have some knowledge of his character and habits and who may have grounds for suspicion that he is not quite right in his mind at times. Such persons would probably be unwilling to communicate suspicions to the Police for fear of trouble or notoriety, whereas if there were a prospect of reward it might overcome their scruples.

Bond had delivered to the inquest and the police, a *profile* of the man responsible for the brutal murders. And whilst it is likely that modern profilers would take exception to one or two ingredients contained in this very brief account of a serial killer, it is nonetheless an important milestone in crime investigation.

It would be almost three quarters of a century later when another eureka moment would take Bond's embryonic psychological autopsy, and add the final piece to the jig saw that would give us the most powerful tool in our modern armoury.

Prior to the investigation and apprehension of Harvey Glatman, for a series of rapes and murders, police officers tended to treat what we now call serial killers, as a number of individual murders. Glatman changed all that. Here was the first of the "signature killers". Here was the man who would provide proof that if the investigation focussed upon the pattern, then prediction could follow. Modern profilers like Robert Ressler and Paul Britton have turned this process into a science of uncanny precision.

Had either Ressler or Britton been around in 1888, or indeed had the Ripper murders been perpetrated today, then the profile picture of our killer would have undoubtedly led to an arrest. Perhaps it would be opportune to speculate as to the likely cause of events had this indeed been the case.

If one removes hindsight from the equation, and looks at the developing pattern of murders in Whitechapel at the relevant time, one must first accept that this is an area in which at least one murder a day is the norm. Two thirds of those murders are committed against men, while the other third find women as the victim. Most murders are committed against or within the poorer classes and it is likely that the doctors of the day – and indeed it was they who dictated much in the way of the investigating officer's response to each crime, would have had greatly varying degrees of competence – and care – when it came to attending the scene of a murder on the streets of Whitechapel. Dr Llewellyn's shoddy performance by the side of poor Polly Nichols is a prime example of this couldn't-care-less attitude. To be turned out in the early hours after a long day earning his not insubstantial crust must have been a real bind. To be then confronted with the bloody body of yet another worthless individual precipitated a quick glance, the pronouncement of life extinct and the issuing of a few instructions designed to get him back to his bed as quickly as possible. Replace him with a modern forensic pathologist (or indeed one of the more enthusiastic city doctors of the time,) then the story may have been very different.

Assuming that prostitute murders previous to that of Emma Elizabeth Smith on 3rd April 1888 can be discounted as being run-of-the mill enquiries for the Metropolitan Police, then it may be that Smith's demise is an ideal place to start our re-examination, using modern thinking and also posing the question: Who was the Ripper? What kind of person was he? Does a man like William Benjamin Belcher fit the profile? For Dianne

Bainbridge and her family, this was probably the most important question.

Using the formulae employed within Behavioural Evidence Analysis, we have to consider much more than just the crime and its victim. The wider background is often the key to unpicking that lock that will put us on the trail of our suspect. That our murder sits within the densely packed conurbation of Whitechapel is of vital importance. Had Smith and the other girls been attacked in Pall Mall or Mayfair, then the story – and police response, would have been greatly different.

It is fair to say that Whitechapel teemed with life; it is also fair to say that once the regular folks had retired for the night, there was still an ever shifting pulse that saw the streets populated with workmen, revellers, criminals and of course prostitutes. As far as the police are concerned, each of the night's travellers is a potential witness; each window that looks out onto the darkness of Flower and Dean Street and Whitechapel Road contains a set of eyes that may, if the right questions are asked at the right time, provide a description of a suspect, or the tiniest lead that will generate a new line of enquiry.

The Judge's Rules that laid down the foundation of good society suggested that all persons had a responsibility to help the police in their endeavours to keep the streets free of criminality. But that help would only be given if the witness felt safe to put pen to paper. When the witness was also the victim, and when she, like Emma Smith, was too terrified to mark her cross on a police statement, then Victorian Justice ground to a shuddering halt. Victimless prosecutions were still over a century away and without that signature there would be no case to answer.

Emma Smith set out on Easter Monday 1888, having no reason to think that her safety would be compromised in any way other than the norm. Prostitution was and still is a dangerous business; men sometimes wanted more than a woman was prepared to give, and even though these girls were hardened to much that the world would throw at them, there was undoubtedly a catalogue of problems within their trade and lifestyle.

That most were alcoholics and would have had their senses dulled by cheap gin was never the best factor for ensuring personal safety – but when the punter's threepence was the only available currency that could be translated into more liquor, or a bed for the night, then what the hell? Common sense is replaced by the basics of need. In addition, once the girl had engaged her dashing beau, the geographical location for the act to be carried out would by necessity require an element of seclusion; a dark alley, a sheltered doorway, or if she was lucky, a quiet passage in one of the crumbling old Whitechapel tenements.

Emma Smith would have known more than her fair share of cranks, violent men and dark alleys, but she would have borne the bruises and the bites and the memories as mere badges of office. What she could not have possibly known as she left her lodgings in George Street, was what, or who lay in wait for her in the early hours.

Fellow lodger Margaret Hayes saw Emma in Farrant Street shortly after midnight talking to a man wearing dark clothing and muffled by a white scarf. By that time, there had already been "some rough work," according to Margaret, indicating that violence had already been witnessed on the streets. In every large city in the world, criminals will, where they can, take control of all money making opportunities and the pimping of prostitutes was and still is a major source of income. Whitechapel had its fair share of young thugs; criminal gangs who preyed on the vulnerable and thought little of dishing out punishment where non compliance or alliance to "the other side" was detected. Indeed Margaret had already been beaten up by two such thugs that night, and it is likely that they were still abroad, looking for more opportunities to flex their collective muscles.

At around half past one, Emma was making her way warily down Whitechapel Road, heading for home, when she saw a group of two or three young men in front of her, near to Whitechapel Church. It is clear that whatever state of mind Emma was in at the time, and despite the fact that it was not unusual to see men hanging around the streets at that hour, alarm bells rang in her head. She crossed over the road in an attempt to avoid them.

Emma Smith must, I believe, have known these men, otherwise she would have given them no more than a sideways glance; she may even have propositioned one or more of their number. That she attempted to avoid them was an indication that their presence represented a clear and imminent danger to her.

The avoidance strategy did not work as Emma had hoped, and the men likewise crossed over the road to approach her. She turned into Osborne Street; they followed. As she approached number 10 Brick Lane, the men pounced, beating her savagely and robbing her of whatever pittance she may have had in her possession at the time. Their parting gift was to drag her down and ram an object deep into her vagina.

As the men turned and left her, no doubt well satisfied with the savagery of their night's work, poor Emma was left to count the cost of their handiwork. In excruciating pain and bleeding heavily from her wounds, she pulled the shawl from her shoulders and pushed it under her skirt, trying to stem the flow of blood until she could reach the safety of her home – just 300 yards away.

According to residents at the George Street Lodging House, it would be sometime between four and five that morning before Emma arrived there, such was the extent of her injuries. It was obvious that the woman needed urgent hospital attention, but anyone in Whitechapel would tell you that if you didn't have money, then the ministrations of medical staff at the Infirmary were more likely to lead to death rather than recovery. Whether or not this was necessarily true is a matter for conjecture, but what is for certain is that since the days of bodysnatching, the poor had a great mistrust of all persons medical.

Another consideration is that Emma would have been highly unlikely to survive her injuries regardless of where she was taken for hospital attention. Having violently breached the wall between vagina and rectum the internal damage was such that faecal peritonitis and other complications were inevitable. Fever conditions would set in rapidly and evidence obtained from her beyond this point would have been worthless.

What she did manage to say to Mary Russell and Annie Lee back at George Street was probably minimal. Emma was an intensely private woman and much of her early life was a mystery. The women noted that she had injuries to her face and that her ear was bleeding. She had clearly been beaten up and during the subsequent half mile walk to the Infirmary, Emma pointed out the location where that assault had taken place.

It is again highly likely that Emma Smith was unable to go into any of the facts surrounding her maltreatment in great detail because of her physical condition and the mental stress that she would have been enduring. Facts were however elicited by the doctor who received her into the Infirmary, and these were written down and later handed to the coroner's officer.

She died at nine o' clock on the morning of 4th April; cause of death: peritonitis. Two days later, courtesy of coroner Wynne E. Baxter, papers relating to the case arrived on the desk of police inspector Edmund Reid. His observations and the resulting questions would have been little different to those of a modern SIO (Senior Investigating Officer).

1. Was the testament given by Smith, albeit hearsay, true?
2. Was the evidence given by her friends accurate and true?
3. What was the relationship that she had, if any, with her assailants?

4. Was there a reason for the assault beyond bad-mindedness?
5. Why did she not report the assault to police constables whom she would have met en route home?
6. Did her journey 300 yards home really take over three hours?
7. Had she or her relatives, including her spouse, any unfinished business with the Whitechapel gangs?
8. What is the likely profile of her attacker(s)

In order to answer any of the questions posed, we have to assume that the information at our disposal is both factual and true. We are on sticky ground from the very beginning.

Emma Smith, according to some sources, was the partner of a wily criminal who went by the pseudonym of Fingers Freddy. Any criminal with a prostitute as a girlfriend would have wanted to control both her and the money that she made. That there were Kray-like organisations within the area, all of whom would have taken exception to a privateer like Freddy working on their turf, would have had only one end result. Either Emma, her boyfriend or both, would have ended up being "warned" about their conduct. Had this indeed been the cause of Smith's demise, (regardless of whether her death had been deliberate, accidental or reckless), the police would never have been provided with statements of evidence in order to identify offenders or prosecute the offence. When one lives in the same streets as those who can deliver punishment at the click of a finger, one does not put pen to paper.

Was she attacked by one man or a gang? Could one man have physically held her down and caused those appalling injuries? Well, the answer to the last question is yes, of course. I have seen the same injuries caused in one-on-one assaults. Delicate tissues take little force to rupture. There was no weapon recovered – a walking stick or a cosh could have quite easily been used. That being the case and had one man been responsible, then why would Emma have told the ladies back at George Street that it was a gang of young men?   Again, the answer is simple - divert attention and survive.

Perhaps this simple fact is reason enough that she chose not to tell any passing policeman her tale of woe. They ask questions. They want to know why and who and where. In addition, all that she would have wanted to do was get back to a place of comfort and safety. Emma Smith may not have known that she was dying, but she knew that help was available in one place and one place only: at home.

That 300 yard journey may have taken five minutes or five hours. It really does not matter, as the evidence surrounding the case is shrouded in confusion and mystery. Of course her injuries were horrendous. If indeed she had crawled home with blood dripping from her wounds and a shawl pushed between her legs and had she passed a constable en route, is it likely that he would have walked past and ignored her? Is it possible that she could have had the wherewithal and the energy to duck into a doorway and conceal herself?

I find it very hard to believe that any police officer would fail to see her and act upon his findings, unless of course he was absolutely sure that there were no witnesses to compromise his position. These were the days when a constable would be dragged unceremoniously out of bed next morning if he missed something tangible on his night shift beat. I know this from personal experience in the 1970s! A broken window, an open door, a dead body. Even if the lad had scrawled a quick pencil note in his pocket book – *saw bleeding woman, told me to naff off, left her to carry on with her journey in view of her refusal to let me help* – he would have done so; covered his back and kept his job. That is the nature of the beast and always has been.

And if our modern SIO had to set about directing operations, what kind of person would be sought? Whether gang or solo, he who committed the monstrous act was no newcomer to criminality; this was almost certainly a brutal individual who had himself been scarred by violence. To become this callous, one needs to have been immersed in brutality oneself. This is a psychopath who enjoys his work. The injury may also be punishment as well as pleasure. "Take this injury home with you, Ms Smith. This is what happens when you cross me."

The French have given us the verb piquer – to prick or stab. From this we derive piquerism: the pleasure obtained in penetration of the skin by stabbing. This pleasure is often sexual. A man who becomes sexually aroused by such activity may not need physical penetration to ejaculate, as the instrument takes the place of his penis. That the Ripper did not, according to post mortem findings, engage in obvious sexual activity with his victims, may well indicate this leaning towards piquerism. Whoever caused Emma Smith's injuries certainly had this in common with the Whitechapel murderer. Sadly there is little evidence available to detail Smith's post mortem examination, which was probably carried out by the house surgeon at the London Hospital, George Haslip. The fact that the cause of death, peritonitis, is given, indicates that the abdomen must have been opened, but further than this we cannot be certain.

That there is also an alleged robbery involved adds an extra ingredient to the Smith case. Why? She would only have had a few pennies on her person anyway. Was this a tax? Was this part and parcel of the pimp-wars that were raging at the time?

He who inflicted the injury was making a statement. Had the wound been in her stomach or chest or had she been slashed across the face with a knife, then it may have said something completely different. Because it was directed to her vaginal region makes it intensely personal and very much of a sexual nature. He was also very confident of one fact. Emma Smith would not name him. There would be no retributions and prosecutions once he walked away from his bleeding victim.

Subsequently, to lay the blame at any one individual, let alone a group of men, is nigh on impossible. The quality of evidence simply does not exist in order that we may do so. But, regardless of our quandary with the Smith case, it is of great significance, as here was the real starting point for the Metropolitan Police to open a case and arouse their collective interests in assaults of this nature. Little did they know what lay ahead.

In fact, **Martha Tabram** lay ahead. Another Public Holiday and another murder. Martha, a 39 year old prostitute with a troubled past and an unhealthy dependence upon alcohol, was just one of hundreds of "unfortunate women" who patrolled Whitechapel's streets, selling their bodies in return for "doss money" and liquor.

After reading contemporary accounts of Martha's murder, and more importantly the police response to it, I can only conclude that the boys in blue did a rather good job, commensurate of course with the nature of policing at that time, in their attempts to track down and bring to justice he, or they who had carried out the murder.

Bearing in mind that almost three quarters of all murders are committed by someone who is known to the victim and with whom there is often a domestic arrangement, then it would have been critical for the Metropolitan Police to identify her corpse as quickly as possible. That her bloodied body screamed of overkill they could hardly have failed to notice. This, to Detective Inspector Edmund Reid would have spelled personal; very personal.

There was no wedding ring; not unusual. If the girl's had possessed such an item it would have been pawned long ago. But somewhere there may still have been a husband or a jealous boyfriend. Get to him quickly and there may yet be evidence in the form of a bloodstained knife or soiled clothing burning in a fire grate.

And then there was the previously mentioned case of Emma Smith and the warring gangs that had lately flexed their muscles and were taxing and murdering with lustful abandon - were the cases linked? It was all very confusing and very untidy. A name would have given the inspector his first roll of the dice. An address and an anxious *significant other* would have been the six that the detective needed to roll in order that enquiries could start in earnest.

The fact that Martha Tabram lay unidentified in the mortuary for a couple of days before she was finally given a name, meant the police were left to follow up information provided to them by a witness whose evidence could be later ripped to shreds by any barrister worth his salt.

"Pearly Poll", or Mary Ann Connelly as the Catholic Church would have known her, was a woman very much in Martha Tabram's own mould: a drink sodden alcoholic who made her living by entertaining any gentleman who had the required assets to ply her with gin and thereafter reap his fumbled reward. It was Poll, who at ten o' clock on the night of 6th August 1888 formed the fourth party in a merry congo of revellers down at the Two Brewers pub on Brick Lane. The other two in their company were soldiers; uniformed and obviously local; one private and one corporal. Martha would probably have been pleasantly drunk by the time that she had acquired her company, for she had been seen some hours before, "quite alone", entering the White Swan in Whitechapel Road.

As Martha and Poll had only known each other a few days, one cannot assume that there would have been any great friendship or intimate knowledge of each other, nor can we assume that any system had been developed for working the punters. The two women may have met by chance that night, both seeking business, but joined by common endeavour. Our uniformed soldiers on the other hand would have travelled together to Whitechapel; for them there would have been an element of planning and two girls rather than one would have been the object of the night's campaign. It may have been that the getting together of our foursome was nothing other than convenience for later copulation.

These facts may seem irrelevant, but in choreographing the hours prior to a murder, one can often find a motive or indeed some organisation that lies before the deed. They are also important, because they lead us to understand why it was that Pearly Poll could give the police no other assistance in relation to formal identification. All that she could offer was a basic description of the soldiers and a guess at the time of events that unfolded.

Poll would tell the police that she and her corporal parted company with Martha and the private at around fifteen minutes before midnight. Poll would take her soldier to Angel Alley in order to carry out her business while Martha was seen heading into Whitechapel.

Activities with the corporal were concluded within thirty minutes, and Poll, who seemed to have no arrangement with Martha for later rendezvous, (further endorsing the casual nature of their association), disappeared into the early hours.

If we now move to the scene of Tabram's murder, we find a narrow alley called George Yard, the dwellings around which are occupied by the poorest class of people. It is within shuffling distance of Whitechapel Road and Angel Alley, so it should not have taken Martha very long to arrive here after leaving Poll. Pearly Poll was to part company with her soldier at the corner of George Yard at around twelve fifteen a.m., so it is likely that both girls went from the bustle of the main thoroughfare no further than was absolutely necessary to ensure some element of privacy in order that activities could be concluded.

The discovery of Martha's body at the dump spot, (the location at which the killer leaves his victim) at around 4.50 a.m., would have been the starting point for Detective Inspector Reid's timeline, a document that would have sat at the top of the enquiry into her death and which would have been constantly referred and added to as the circumstances surrounding her demise were uncovered. In fact, as information was so reluctantly given, there were precious few entries of any real value.

11.45 p.m. 6th August: Following earlier sightings in company with Pearly Poll and the soldiers, the two couples part company near Angel Alley.

1.50 a.m. 7th August, Elizabeth Mahoney, a resident in George Yard Buildings returns to her dwelling. She notes no one in the vicinity.

2.00 a.m. 7th August. Police Constable Barrett sees a Grenadier Guardsman at the north end of George Yard. The soldier explains his presence there as "waiting for a chum who has gone off with a girl." Nothing about the soldier alerts any suspicion in the officer.

2.30 a.m. – 2.45 a.m. 7th August: Martha Tabram is killed.

3.30 a.m. 7th August, Alfred Crow returns to his dwelling in George Yard Buildings. He notices a body on the stairs, but as to whether it is alive or dead he is unable to say. Dossers – homeless vagrants are not uncommon in this area, so Alfred would be unlikely to investigate further.

4.45 a.m. 7th August, John Reeves, another resident, returns home and discovers (probably the same) body on the upper landing of the Yard. The first light of dawn is spreading over London and he is able to discern a pool of blood under the body. He runs off to fetch a policeman without examining the corpse.

Upon Police Constable Barrett returning with Reeves, the enquiry clicks into gear. A police surgeon estimates time of death at between 2.30 and 2.45 a.m. His estimations would be based upon the progression of rigor mortis, which normally commences around two hours following death in the small muscles of the face and finger ends, before travelling down to the rest of the body. Algor mortis, or body temperature, may also have been taken into consideration, although with the great loss of blood that Martha seems to have suffered, this may not have been such a reliable means of calculation.

A matter of immediate concern for the police would have been the identity of the soldier seen by Constable Barrett: Was this the same individual who had earlier been entertained by Pearly Poll? If this was indeed the case, then, although Martha's entertaining had taken considerably longer than the fifteen minutes to half an hour that sex in the streets would have normally taken, there was a likelihood that her private was the very same as he who had been seen with her earlier that morning. And of crucial importance, if the doctor's estimations were correct, then this soldier was still with her at the time of her death.

It is little wonder that the detectives carried out such thorough enquiries, including a number of identification parades at local barracks – all of which produced little of credible evidential value. Indeed, Pearly Poll would turn the whole process into a farce by first failing to attend the identification parades and then, adding as much music hall comedy to proceedings as she could possibly muster. That the final parade did not take place until 13th August, almost a week later, tells its own story.

The Bradford Observer, in an article dated 14th August 1888, tells us: *The murder of the young woman supposed to be Martha Turner, which occurred at George Yard Buildings, Whitechapel Road, London, is as much a* mystery as ever, and up to the present there is no decided clue as to the perpetrator of the foul crime. The woman who was seen in the company of two soldiers, with whom was the deceased, has not been able to identify either of the men at the Tower as being her companion on the evening of the murder.

Inspector Reid and the other officers engaged in the case have in no way relaxed their efforts to trace the criminal, and yesterday, the inspector, accompanied by "Pearly Poll", who was in the company of the murdered woman, proceeded to the Tower, where she was confronted with every non-commissioned officer and private who had leave of absence at the time of the outrage.

They were paraded at the back of the Tower, unseen by the public, and "Pearly Poll" was asked, "Can you see either of the men you saw with the woman now dead?" "Pearly Poll," in no way embarrassed, placed her arms akimbo, glanced at the men with the air of an inspecting officer, and shook her head. This indication of a negative was not sufficient. "Can you identify anyone?" she was asked. "Pearly Poll" exclaimed, with a good deal of feminine emphasis "He ain't here". The woman was very decided on this point, and the men were then dismissed, while the two upon whom a faint shadow of suspicion had rested were considerably relieved at their innocence being declared.

As soon as the murder was known, the suspected Corporal was interviewed by the police and questioned. He had his bayonet with him when on leave at the time of the outrage; but this he at once produced, and no trace of

50

blood was discovered upon it. His clothing, too, was also examined, and upon it there was no incriminating bloodstain. After the parade, Adjutant Cotton, the officer in command, stated that all the men were now entirely exonerated. Indeed, the men were themselves most anxious to afford every facility to the police, and gave all the information in their power to assist the officers of justice in their investigation.

Pearly Poll, who was very likely drunk at the time of the killing, (and probably inebriated to some degree at the time of the ID parade), had ensured that the only thing to come from Tabram's death was the raising of her own celebrity. Once again, the value of evidence gathered by the main witness was negligible.

Constable Barrett also attended an identification parade in company with Detective Inspector Reid and despite picking out two men; the detective would dismiss his selection as next to worthless. Thus, without any value in the testimony of the witnesses, there only remained the injuries inflicted upon Tabram to convey, if they could, any clue as to the author of her death.

Martha Tabram had been stabbed thirty nine times, the concentration of her wounds being around the breasts, abdomen, stomach and vagina. Internal organ damage had been suffered and the cause of death was given as penetration of her heart. The weapon used, according to Dr. Timothy Keleen, was an ordinary penknife, the blades of which, in those days, were around three inches in length. There were two anomalies in the matter of injuries and weapon: While the stabbing had been carried out by a right handed perpetrator, one of the injuries was, said the doctor, the work of a knife held in the left hand. Similarly, one wound among those inflicted had been caused by a longer and stouter bladed weapon than the penknife. (Again, no detailed post mortem report is available to assist us.)

So, could two men have been responsible? Perhaps private soldier one invites the corporal back to view his handiwork and number two adds a token stab on his own? Could the penknife blade have broken or cut into the murderer's hand, causing him to swap hands and add a final blow with another weapon?

Could the surgeon have been mistaken?

Martha Tabram had, according to Constable Barrett, been left in a position which showed that she had recently engaged in intimacy. She was on her back, her legs were open and no attempt had been made to cover up the dead woman's dignity. Her clothes had been left in disarray, *as if she had had a struggle with someone*, according to witness John Reeves. No evidence of ejaculate was found upon her or within the vagina. (Not unusual, as prostitutes were very wily in their ability to simulate penetration with their fingers. But, such simulation would generally be more effective while the girls were standing against a wall or bending forward to allow access from the rear, according to contemporary prostitutes.)

This left even more speculation for the police: Had penetration not been possible for some reason? Had our man snapped due to his dysfunction? Had the girl said something to him to cause him to snap? (The male ego is fragile indeed in the matter of his sexual ability – or lack of it – and this has often been the cause of a frenzied murder or two.)

Too many loose ends; too many questions that could never be answered; and worst of all – a police *own goal* that would finish off the enquiry for good. Events were, for reasons best known to the uniformed hierarchy, shrouded in a Masonic veil of secrecy. Hardly anything of value was shared with the press and public. The former whinged, the latter lost interest and Martha Tabram's death soon became the stuff of chip paper.

Time and time again it was found that the upper echelons of the service, often drafted in from the military rather than having served their time on the front lines of policing, would make decisions that would baffle the foot soldiers, who as mentioned, did their best to solve this crime. Those unfathomable decisions may have also allowed Jack to kill again...and again.

Profiling? Too many inconsistencies to be of value.

Mary Ann (Polly) Nichols: Nothing Personal me owld cock...

Jack the Ripper's killing career did not start on the streets of London, of that I can be quite certain. The first time that he plunged a knife into someone's abdomen or sliced open a throat was many years before; not in Whitechapel's cobbled alleys, but in the dark shadows of his own mind.

Jack would have always been a one-off; a man like him could have slipped in and out of a crowd and laughed and joked with the best of them down at the Frying Pan or the White Swan, but he would have known since childhood that he was different to the rest; special in so many ways. He could not and would not have discussed his sexual fantasies down at the pub while his mates were lewdly chatting up some unfortunate whom they were plying with drink, for they would not understand the inner workings of his mind; only he would be able to sort out the tangle of emotions, desires and sexual triggers that drove him. Things like this were best kept to himself; pondered over as he walked through the streets in the early hours, acted out in moments of tormented privacy, and incorporated carefully into the grand plan when the day eventually came for its execution. That day was the 30th August 1888. And execution is a very apt description.

A hedonistic killer like Jack does not select his victim with any degree of care or personal connection. He selects her from a group; a group with whom he can easily have access and whose members are unlikely to raise the roof when lewd solicitations are made. That group are prostitutes.

For a few pennies they can be encouraged to hide with you in the shadows, lift up their petticoats and allow you to act out your every fantasy. In just a few minutes and for the price of no more than a glass or two of gin, you can achieve the same rewards that years of courtship earns you in a normal relationship.

While her customer relieves the frustrations of months at sea, plays with the parts that his wife will not let him or simply acts out a fantasy or two, she throws back her head and watches the gulls soaring over the rooftops. She juggles the copper coins in her hand and listens idly to the sounds of the carriages on Whitechapel Road or the screams of starving kids behind the same wall that supports the weight of both she and her busy little client.

She may groan and tell him that he is the most wonderful lover she has ever known; she may encourage his climax with kind words and thrusts of her hips, but the truth is, she has no more connection with him than he has with her. It is all just business; a necessity of life; just as murder is for Jack.

Mary Ann Nichol's movements in the hours prior to her death are, in the main, rather sketchy. Our timeline would leave stitches dropped here and there and would give us little to indicate the author of her demise. That she ate and drank and serviced her clients in the oppressive heat of a thundery night are accepted. That she was seen bouncing off walls in inebriation, laughing and joking with her friend is nothing more than the first step in a journey that would lead to her death. She was quite simply in the wrong place at the wrong time when she made her way north from Whitechapel Road to the quieter roads and streets beyond.

One wonders why she strayed from the busier thoroughfare; after all, if there were customers to be had, then surely it would have been better to remain where she was? Up in Buck's Row there was a corner pub and a few commercial premises, but predominantly that street consisted of dwelling houses. A suggestion had been made in local newspapers that on the morning of Mary's death a woman had been heard screaming murder and running towards Buck's Row. It was further reported that this individual sounded as if she was carrying an injury, as her voice sounded laboured. Had Mary been chased from Whitechapel Road, or was this just part of her normal perambulations?

Once again, it is hard to elicit the truth as so much evidence has been lost or stolen from police repositories, but other reports suggest that residents in Buck's Row, light sleepers among them, heard not a whisper. With this in mind, it would be useful to view the full post mortem report, as the state of Nichols' rigor mortis may have told a tale or two. As previously mentioned, rigor will normally commence after two hours – quicker during these hot summer months – in the small muscles of the face. It will then travel down the body at a fairly predictable rate until full rigor is achieved between twelve and eighteen hours after death. A victim who ran for a good distance prior to their death, may, according to pathologists, have rigor that commences in the large muscles of the legs, as these will be depleted of oxygen, and therefore be prone to speedier onset. We therefore have to rely upon a decent pathologist who will carry out a full and careful examination of the corpse in order that we might determine this fact, and thereby the victim's immediate pre death activity. We will learn that in Nichol's case this was never going to happen.

We know that Mary Ann was seen by her friend Emily Holland, at 2.30 a.m. having just come down Osborn Street onto the main road. She tells Emily, whom she meets outside of a grocer's shop on the corner of Osborn Street and Whitechapel Road that she will solicit one more customer and get her doss money. She will not be long, she adds before heading east along Whitechapel Road. Buck's Row lay at the north side of the road, behind a row of terraced properties, and was accessed via any one of five points between Baker's Row and Brady Street. No one would see her before around 3.40 a.m. when her body was discovered by car man Charles Cross, who is on his way to work.

Cross, prior to investigating the matter further was to summon a passing gentleman, Robert Paul, probably as much for Dutch courage than anything else and tentatively they examine the woman's body. They cannot be sure if Mary is still breathing, or if a pulse can be discerned. (This is not unusual. From my own experience I have found that a corpse lying in the flickering shadows of night may give the appearance of breathing. Also, without training and suitable equipment, even the faintest pulse is hardly discernible.) They run off to fetch Police Constable Mizen, but in the meanwhile two more police officers arrive at the scene, and from this point we must pay close attention to the proceedings that follow.

At this point, there will drop into gear, a well rehearsed procedure for dealing with a suspicious death enquiry, note-taking and the summoning of a senior officer and police surgeon included. The latter will, as was always the case in Victorian murder investigations, direct the initial actions. It is incumbent upon the surgeon to gather as much evidence as is possible before ordering the removal of the body to the nearest mortuary. As Dr. Rees Llewellyn was being hammered from his slumbers and walks a third of a mile to the scene, the officers guarding the corpse are making careful note of what they see. Despite the fact that she is clearly beyond revival, they are not authorised to pronounce life extinct. Had her head been lying at the opposite side of the street, still they would not be qualified to use the D word. Llewellyn alone that night would possess that power.

Mary Ann Nichols, throat gaping wipe, is lying on her back; her skirts which had been raised, exposing her genital area, had been pulled down by Cross and Paul in order to preserve the woman's dignity. Both of these men would have been early suspects and would need quickly to be eliminated from suspicion.

Police Constable John Neil, one of the two officers who stumbled upon the body when Messrs Paul and Cross leave it, seems to have carried out a most proficient examination of the scene, particularly looking for evidence of blood transfer. He sees no footsteps or wheel marks. He feels the woman's arms and they appear to be warm, indicating that death was most recent. It seems that the woman had been murdered where she lay. Significantly, regardless of the openly displayed genitalia, this footpath adjacent to dwelling houses was not a place where sex would have taken place, adding to the confusion left behind by the murderer.

Dr. Llewellyn's arrival at 4 a.m. would have been welcomed by the officers guarding the body, but his cursory and almost derisory examination of the victim and location would leave them astounded. He feels her face and arms, presumably trying to establish the presence of rigor mortis; presumably he finds no stiffness as he concludes that she had been dead less than an hour. Her face is quite cold, but bearing in mind that she would have had lost a few pints of blood via the wound to her neck, this is to be expected.

Confounding those watching, the doctor orders Nichol's removal to the mortuary and heads back home to arms of Morpheus. The constables would have at least expected Nichols to be lifted and an examination of what lay beneath to be carried out. What if there had been a knife sticking out the woman's vertebrae? What if the blood evidence beneath her had a story to tell?

It is left to the officers to note the small circle of congealed blood under the corpse and the trickle running down to the gutter. Their hands are bloodied in hauling the corpse onto the wheelbarrow that serves as ambulance; a point that is noted and later delivered in evidence.

Once at the mortuary, Shift Inspector John Spratling assumes responsibility for the progress of the enquiry. While waiting outside for the keys to arrive, he notes for the first time the wounds to Nichol's abdomen. Llewellyn is once more hammered from his slumbers and will make his earlier than anticipated appearance and post mortem examination. Before he arrives however, the pauper inmates who serve as mortuary assistants strip and wash the body. Vast amounts of evidence are hereby lost.

Dr Llewellyn will later note:

"Five teeth were missing, and there was a slight laceration of the tongue. There was a bruise running along the lower part of the jaw on the right side of the face. That might have been caused by a blow from a fist or pressure from a thumb. There was a circular bruise on the left side of the face which also might have been inflicted by the pressure of the fingers. On the left side of the neck, about 1 in. below the jaw, there was an incision about 4 in. in length, and ran from a point immediately below the ear. On the same side, but an inch below, and commencing about 1 in. in front of it, was a circular incision, which terminated at a point about 3 in. below the right jaw. That incision completely severed all the tissues down to the vertebrae. The large vessels of the neck on both sides were severed. The incision was about 8 in. in length. The cuts must have been caused by a long-bladed knife, moderately sharp, and used with great violence. No blood was found on the breast, either of the body or the clothes. There were no injuries about the body until just about the lower part of the abdomen. Two or three inches from the left side was a wound running in a jagged manner. The wound was a very deep one, and the tissues were cut through. There were several incisions running across the abdomen. There were three or four similar cuts running downwards, on the right side, all of which had been caused by a knife which had been used violently and downwards. The injuries were from left to right and might have been done by a left handed person. All the injuries had been caused by the same instrument."

Comparing events above to modern murder investigations, one is left with various thoughts:

1. The police of the day seem to have done a very thorough job. From the constables at the dump spot who note and record relevant facts, notifying thereafter the relevant authorities in the correct order and manner, through to the inspector and detectives who would accelerate the enquiry.
2. The murder scene itself is shown an alarming lack of attention. Where now we may leave the scene undisturbed for days or weeks, the whole Nichol's affair is over in an hour or so. Even before Inspector Spratling gets to the scene and appraises himself of issues relating to the offence, someone has swilled water on the footpath and washed away all but crevices of blood in the cracks of the pavement. He carries out a search of the surrounding area but notes nothing of interest.
3. Techniques and procedures were simply not in place in those days for the collection of evidence, and it would not be until Sir Bernard Spilsbury's intervention well into the 20th century before the scene was afforded proper respect as a repository of vital evidence.
4. It is accepted that much evidence has been spirited away over the years, so there may be

more – much more that a retrospective detective could ponder upon. As it is, we are left with precious little.

5. Dr. Llewellyn, for reasons best known to himself, seems to be more concerned with getting back to his bed rather than squeezing every last shred of evidence from the murder scene. Later murder enquiries in the Ripper series, particularly those in the wealthier City of London, would show how the Nichol's scene should have properly been handled.

And so, what of the offender and the circumstances of the offence? Mary Ann Nichols is targeted within an hour or so of leaving her friend Emily Holland. She has had sex with numerous men that night and is according to her own admission soliciting one more in order to secure the money for her lodgings. She is clearly not at the scene of a sexual encounter and nor does it appear that she has found her fee paying beau, yet the position in which her body is left has very clear sexual connotations.

There are many possible explanations for events leading up to her death and the geographical position of her body.

- Mary had been chased from nearby streets, corroborating some reports in local newspapers of a disturbance and a fleeing woman. She has been effectively silenced by the cutting of her throat, a method employed in later murders to excellent effect. (This single injury was more than likely that which detectives used as the differentiation between this and murders that went before.) If those injuries had been inflicted first, then Mary would have died within a few minutes, but after initial blood loss, would have been too weak to do other than watch helplessly as her assailant carried out the knife-work on her body. Serial killers who fall within the hedonistic lust category would find the greatest pleasure in seeing the terror in a victim's eyes. For him there would be no greater demonstration of his power over the girl;

- She may have also been heading to a location for sex with her customer, showing that she had psychologically assessed him and was happy with any risk. (Thus indicating the nature of her chap, who would have fallen within the "average Joe" classification.)
- She may have been approached silently and attacked without any warning or sight of her assailant. Once again, having had her throat cut, she would have made no noise other than gurgling - and that made as she fell to, and writhed on the ground.
- The injuries inflicted upon Mary Ann's body are extreme indeed, going much further than those one finds in the average murder. That the killer, once he has silenced his victim, then concentrates immediately and solely upon the lower abdominal / genital area is a clear statement of intent. This is personal to him. That the edge of the main wound is described as jagged may also be very significant.

It could of course indicate that the murderer has had to hack through layers of clothing or that his victim was struggling beneath him when he was carrying out his attack, but it could also signify that she had been writhing beneath him, quite alive as the attack is carried out.

- The fact that there are other knife marks on her body which do not seem to have any purpose other than decoration may also be statement as to the killer's task interpretation and state of mind.
- The lack of blood around our murder scene shows that the killer has thought this crime out very carefully. A severed carotid artery will spurt blood immediately after the initial wound unless steps are taken to stem that flow. Had Nichols been standing when the wound was inflicted, one would have expected to find some evidence of blood loss on the pavement around her, separate to that which was lost as she lay on the ground. That there is none was and still is a cause of great debate.
- It is likely, in my opinion, that the spot in which Mary was found was that at which she was murdered.

And what of the profile of this individual? We first need to establish a link between the previous murders of Smith and Tabram. Police at that time considered that they fell into the Whitechapel stabbing group, thereby warranting further rigorous investigation, but links were not made. (This is still an area of great contention, but the modus operandi, locations and likelihood of the victim being at, or near a place where sex was to take place are all very different. Emma Smith – not at scene and apparently attacked by a group. Martha Tabram at known scene of sexual activity. Mary Nichols, not at scene of sexual activity.) Likewise the injuries, extreme though they may be, are also varied enough to give us more cause to separate rather than link the two crimes. Tabram is stabbed. Nichols is cut. The latter tells us a lot more about our man. He has a clear purpose. Stabbing can be frenzied, fuelled by hatred and beyond the mental control of an assailant. Cutting suggests a far more complex motive. He does not just want his victim to die, he is disfiguring her, destroying her identity as a human being and exercising the ultimate power and control over her.

Mary Ann Nichol's murderer would therefore need to be considered for profiling on the basis of one crime, separate from that of Smith and Tabram. But, significantly, the extreme nature of the crime forces us to acknowledge that this may well be number one in a series and he would therefore need to be profiled as a serial killer. In short, no one ever gets this mad, commits such an horrendous act, gets away with it and ends his career there and then. Our man has been building up to this murder for years. It is likely that he has killed before, but more significantly he will want more – and very soon too.

A profile carried out on the Ripper in 1988 by F.B.I. agent John Douglas, and recently released in British newspapers states:

'We would look for someone below or above average in height and or weight. (He) May have problems with

speech, scarred complexion, physical illness, or injury. We would not expect this type of offender to be married. If he was married in the past, it would have been to someone older than himself and the marriage would have been for a short duration."

The statement regarding the Ripper's single status does not, I feel, take into account society in Victorian England. Of the hundreds of contemporary murders that I have researched, it would seem that divorce on the grounds of a man's cruelty was a rare event. Women of lower classes married because they needed to, in order to survive. That they could afford to be choosy never entered the equation.

One wonders too, if Victorian prostitutes operated using similar social radars that most modern sex workers do. If the man has overt traits that make him scary or if there is a great likelihood that he may use violence, they will put in place some mechanism for survival, the simplest of which is to decline his offer or withhold any solicitation that she would have made to a "safer" individual.

Agent Douglas continues:

"He is not adept in meeting people socially and the major extent of his heterosexual relationships would be with prostitutes. This offender does not look out of the ordinary. However, the clothing he wears at the time of the assaults is not his everyday dress. He wants to project to unsuspecting females prostitutes that he has money...

'He comes from a family where he was raised by a domineering mother and weak, passive father. In all

likelihood, his mother drank heavily and enjoyed the company of many men.

'As a result, he failed to receive consistent care and contact with stable adult role models.'

Douglas notes that this unstable family background resulted in the killer internalising his anger from his younger years, becoming an introvert and venting his frustration through violent destructive acts. He suggests that the criminal would seek work in a profession where he could be alone and explore his disturbing fantasies imagining him as a butcher or mortician's assistant.

The FBI agent adds *'He would be perceived as being quiet, a loner, shy, slightly withdrawn, obedient, and neat and orderly in appearance and when working. He drinks in the local pubs and after a few spirits, he becomes more relaxed and finds it easier to engage in conversation. He lives or works in the Whitechapel area.'*

I also struggle with the physical description given – scarred, physical injury or illness, and then, in what seems like a contradiction, adding that our man is normal in appearance. If one takes into account the descriptions provided by witnesses of a gentleman of average height, moustache, dressed in contemporary fashion – not one witness describes anything out of the norm.

Later witnesses like Joseph Lavende who see a male suspect chatting with Catherine Eddowes paint a picture of a man who is more than comfortable in the company of women; the kind who, like Ted Bundy, Fred West or Reginald Christie can use their social skills to good and devastating effect when selecting, engaging and luring a victim to her death.

Perhaps the best profile, and one that was reinforced by later murders, is as follows:

Fitting in with the accepted age group attributed to sexually motivated serial killers, he is aged between 25 and 35 years of age. He is an organized killer, local to the murders and is able to fit in and survive a Whitechapel that is very different to that of today. He can hold his own with men and women, can slip in and out of the streets with ease and confidence.

He is able to plan his attacks in a cold and calculating way; selecting his victims from a particular group. He takes with him a weapon, a knife, which tells us that he does not mind being close to his victims. He is comfortable in their presence and is not shocked by seeing the savagery of such butchery.

He is able to converse intelligently with his victims and solicit them, or indeed respond to their overtures should the offering of services be made to him. His appearance would be such that the victims would not be alarmed. He has the presence of mind to walk with his victims to a place where sex could be undertaken. That there is no evidence of sexual activity upon or within the bodies of his victims would reinforce the fact that he is using a ruse in order to get them to their place of execution. He is believable and confident in his transactions. He can persuade later victims, despite the huge police operation and activities in the area - as well as raised public awareness – that he is safe; not the monster who is being sought.

His control and purpose would also suggest that he is sober during the attacks. A drunken man could not carry out such delicate handiwork and slip away unseen into the night without making a mistake or two. His work needs a much practiced hand and a very cool countenance. It is more likely that he was not picking up the girls in public houses, but that he stays on the streets where he is safer.

His handiwork and anatomical knowledge, the extent of which we cannot gauge beyond the fact that he is more than competent, indicates that he has delved into innards before, possibly as a mortuary attendant or butcher; he is very comfortable being bloodied in this way.

He is a psychopath with a deep hatred of women or prostitutes in particular. He is likely to have killed before. He is also likely to have known or been around petty crime since his younger days. He is likely to be socially adequate, with friends, lovers, wife and children.

He is forensically aware. (Contemporary criminals would know just how much evidence could, or more importantly, could not be collected from the scene of a murder. They would not have been bothered by leaving bodily fluids or fingerprints behind, but would have taken care with items that could be identified as being personal to them, particularly weapons and trinkets. The Ripper has knowledge of methods employed by the police, and very likely the timings and locations of their beats. He knows that he has a window of opportunity within which he can safely operate.)

As for fitting the profile to Dianne Bainbridge's ancestor, William Benjamin Belcher, we can indeed tick some of the boxes, but we need more evidence in order to give him a credible position on the list of suspects. For those who are not familiar with the subsequent murders, it may be worth revisiting the relevant facts before looking further at Mr. Belcher and the evidence that would come to light as Dianne tried to further distance her man from the streets of Whitechapel.

Annie Chapman

It would take mental gymnastics of Olympian proportions to imagine that rip number one went

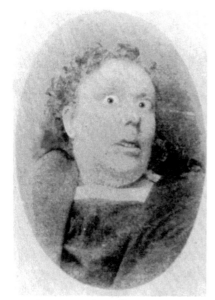

according to plan; that Polly Nichol's murder was just as Jack intended. If Jack was in any way a reflective practitioner then he would have sat at home after the murder and cursed his luck. That just wasn't how it was supposed to be; in the middle of a residential street with nosey neighbours, wandering workmen and bobbies on the prowl. The whole affair was just too messy; there was too much risk and worst of all it was over too damned quickly.

If we know anything at all about Jack, then we have to admit that he was a perfectionist. He was process focussed and if the first plan either didn't work or wasn't how he had imagined it then he would just write it off as a bad job and try again. The darkness and the shadows were where he would have lain in wait and watched. Not for him the pubs with their gas lamps and inquisitive locals. The more who see you and pass the time of day, the more who recognise you and the greater the chance of getting "buckled", to use his own words. And another consideration when it came to imagining him chatting up his victims in the local pub, Jack would have been stone cold sober as he carried out his handiwork; one could not slit throats and execute such delicate operations with beer swilling about in one's belly and one's brains less than crystal clear. Forget about all of this courtship business; this spending of good silver to loosen up your floozy. When the time was right the perfect candidate would chance along – it was meant to be. No need to go looking – that was too messy for Jack.

There is little doubt that in the weeks between Nichols and his next victim, the lad would have been on the streets eyeing up prospective targets; fine tuning locations and times and opportunities, waiting for the perfect time and place to strike. Waiting for Annie Chapman.

When Annie Chapman's mutilated body was found in the early hours of Saturday 8th September, the event further served to reinforce the profile attributed to their unknown and as yet unnamed killer. Had they thought that Nichol's demise was a one-off, perpetrated by some madman who would disappear into oblivion then they were very much mistaken. And as for Jack, if he had given the first of his ventures in infamy any thought, then he had recognised the shortcomings in his method of operation. Number two would be very different indeed.

Chapman, according to her friends back at Crossingham's Lodging House in Dorset Street, was not a well woman. Not only had she been battered in a dispute with a fellow lodger, but she had spent the last few nights in the Infirmary. In all probability her death at the hands of the Ripper was no more than a foreshortening of a lifeline that was coming rapidly to its end in any case.

As it was, her poor health and her past life were of little consequence to her killer; she was not chosen because of who she was, she was chosen because of where she was and what she was. Likewise her past life is of no consequence to us. Suffice to say that she was a prostitute, a heavy drinker and a lodging house dweller who needed a handful of copper to secure a bed for the night. Drink she had already consumed courtesy of previous customers. Shortly after 1.35 a.m. on 8th September, Chapman left the lodging house for the final time, telling night-watchman John Evans to make sure that her bed was kept for her. Chapman promised to return shortly. Her bed at Crossingham's was number 29, a number that would prove to be highly significant before the first light of dawn descended upon old London.

At 5.30 a.m. a 47 year old cart-minder by the name of Elizabeth Long saw someone whom she thought to be Chapman standing with her back hard against the shutters of 29 Hanbury Street. A small man with dark hair was facing her and was engaging her in friendly conversation. "Will you?" he asked. Chapman replied, "Yes."

A few feet from where they were standing was the door to number 29. The door, which was never locked, led directly through to a dingy passage leading to the rear yard. This passage was the only way into the yard so it must be assumed that within a few minutes of Long's sighting, the pair had slipped quietly within in order that the transaction may take place. At 6 o' clock, John Davis, a resident at 29 Hanbury Street went out into the yard and found Chapman's mutilated body. If Elizabeth Long's sighting and her later identification at the mortuary were to be believed, the Ripper had less than thirty minutes to slit Chapman's throat, lift her skirts, mutilate her body and disappear into the dawn. This time there had been no mistake.

Dr. George Bagster Philips arrived at the scene half an hour after the discovery of Chapman's body and in a shift from the disrespect shown by Dr. Llewellyn, afforded the victim his proper and thorough attentions. His observations (although official papers have long since been misappropriated, newspaper reports still exist) were recorded thus:

"The left arm was placed across the left breast. The legs were drawn up, the feet resting on the ground, and the knees turned outwards. The face was swollen and turned on the right side. The tongue protruded between the front teeth, but not beyond the lips. The tongue was evidently much swollen. The front teeth were perfect as far as the first molar, top and bottom and very fine teeth they were. The body was terribly mutilated...the stiffness of the limbs was not marked, but was evidently commencing. He noticed that the throat was dissevered deeply; that the incisions through the skin were jagged and reached right round the neck...On the wooden paling between the yard in question and the next, smears of blood, corresponding to where the head of the deceased lay, were to be seen. These were about 14 inches from the ground, and immediately above the part where the blood from the neck lay.

He should say that the instrument used at the throat and abdomen was the same. It must have been a very sharp knife with a thin narrow blade, and must have been at least 6 in. to 8 in. in length, probably longer. He should say that the injuries could not have been inflicted by a bayonet or a sword bayonet. They could have been done by such an instrument as a medical man used for post-mortem purposes, but the ordinary surgical cases might not contain such an instrument. Those used by the slaughtermen, well ground down, might have caused them. He thought the knives used by those in the leather trade would not be long enough in the blade. There were indications of anatomical knowledge...he should say that the deceased had been dead at least two hours, and probably more, when he first saw her; but it was right to mention that it was a fairly cool morning, and that the body would be more apt to cool rapidly from its having lost a great quantity of blood. There was no evidence...of a struggle having taken place. He was positive the deceased entered the yard alive...

A handkerchief was round the throat of the deceased when he saw it early in the morning. He should say it was not tied on after the throat was cut."

Report following the post mortem examination:

"He noticed the same protrusion of the tongue. There was a bruise over the right temple. On the upper eyelid there was a bruise, and there were two distinct bruises, each the size of a man's thumb, on the forepart of the top of the chest. The stiffness of the limbs was now well marked. There was a bruise over the middle part of the bone of the right hand. There was an old scar on the left of the frontal bone. The stiffness was more noticeable on the left side, especially in the fingers, which were partly closed. There was an abrasion over the ring finger, with distinct markings of a ring or rings. The throat had been severed as before described. The incisions into the skin indicated that they had been made from the left side of the neck. There were two distinct clean cuts on the left side of the spine. They were parallel with each other and separated by about half an inch. The muscular structures appeared as though an attempt had been made to separate the bones of the neck. There were various other mutilations to the body, but he was of the opinion that they occurred subsequent to the death of the woman, and to the large escape of blood from the division of the neck.

The deceased was far advanced in disease of the lungs and membranes of the brain, but they had nothing to do with the cause of death. The stomach contained little food, but there was not any sign of fluid. There was no appearance of the deceased having taken alcohol, but there were signs of great deprivation and he should say she had been badly fed. He was convinced she had not taken any strong alcohol for some hours before her death. The injuries were certainly not self-inflicted. The bruises on the face were evidently recent, especially about the chin and side of the jaw, but the bruises in front of the chest and temple were of longer standing - probably of days. He was of the opinion that the person who cut the deceased throat took hold of her by the chin, and then commenced the incision from left to right. He thought it was highly probable that a person could call out, but with regard to an idea that she might have been gagged he could only point to the swollen face and the protruding tongue, both of which were signs of suffocation.

The abdomen had been entirely laid open: the intestines, severed from their mesenteric attachments, had been lifted out of the body and placed on the shoulder of the corpse; whilst from the pelvis, the uterus and its appendages with the upper portion of the vagina and the posterior two thirds of the bladder, had been entirely removed. No trace of these parts could be found and the incisions were cleanly cut, avoiding the rectum, and dividing the vagina low enough to avoid injury to the cervix uteri. Obviously the work was that of an expert - of one, at least, who had such knowledge of anatomical or pathological examinations as to be enabled to secure the pelvic organs with one sweep of the knife, which must therefore have at least 5 or 6 inches in length, probably more. The appearance of the cuts confirmed him in the opinion that the instrument, like the one which divided the neck, had been of a very sharp character. The mode in which the knife had been used seemed to indicate great anatomical knowledge.

He thought (that) he himself could not have performed all the injuries he described, even without a struggle, in under a quarter of an hour. If he had done it in a deliberate way such as would fall to the duties of a surgeon it probably would have taken him the best part of an hour."

Regardless of the shenanigans that followed, there are a number of observations that are important in the identification of our suspect and in particular the evidence of Elizabeth Long. Much was read into Long's description of the male seen with Chapman, but the fact is that she only saw the back of his head. She was unable to describe whiskers or any facial peculiarities or features. Quite simply, the man was below average height and had dark hair. We must forget the "foreign appearance" and later attribution to the Ripper being Jewish. Such evidence today would be laughed out of court. As a forensic artist I would certainly be unable to recreate more than an individual's clothing and hair viewed from the rear.

Long does help in that she describes a pleasant and confident transaction. This further endorses our man as being sober in his operations and more than capable in engaging his victim. Had Chapman (and Bagster Philips finds little evidence of drunkenness) felt otherwise, then she would surely have called out to Long for help of some kind.

Consider also the position in which the body was left. The left arm was laid across the left breast. This is very significant and when we choreograph the moments prior to the fatal attack, we see just why.

Let us take our couple back to the front of 29 Hanbury Street. The solicitation has been successful; terms and location for the act have been agreed upon and Jack, ever the gentleman, allows Annie to enter the passageway first. He follows behind and in the darkness, as they quietly tip toe towards the back yard, he removes the knife from its place of concealment. As Annie pushes open the back door and carefully climbs down the two sandstone steps into yard, her eyes search out a spot in which to comfortably afford her customer the privileges that he has agreed to pay for. She is now at her most vulnerable and Jack takes full advantage. He grabs her by the hair and in one well rehearsed movement; reaches around to slice open her throat, pulling her head forward as he does so, ensuring thereby that blood does not spurt untidily out into the yard. He holds her in his vice like grip until her blood pressure drops and she, faint with shock and blood loss, goes limp in his arms. He now walks slowly backwards, laying Annie on the flags before him; once she is laid on her back he is free to walk around her body, his footsteps unsoiled by her blood. He lifts her skirts to begin the mutilation that is the object of the exercise.

Had Annie been dead when her body was lowered on the flags, then both arms would have fallen to her sides. It would have been quite impossible for one arm to remain on her breast – gravity would simply not allow it. Choreograph this yourself - with a willing partner of course; the result will always be the same.

Annie Chapman was very much alive when her beau was cutting open her abdomen and carefully removing those parts that he desired. Some speculate that, in those last minutes of life she reached forward and tried to grab his arm; to stop him from cutting away at the soft flesh...until of course she could muster strength to do no more than breathe her last. It was then, with the sweet relief of death upon her that her arm dropped upon her breast and there remained as the Ripper completed his task.

Dr. Bagster Philips, at Annie's inquest, estimates that the time taken by the Ripper to accomplish his operation was up to an hour. But Jack had slit her throat and butchered Chapman in much less than thirty minutes – without waiting for his victim to die it could have been done in around fifteen minutes flat. If you ever watch a slaughter man trying to make his bonus you will see how quickly a body can be stripped of both life and parts. And Jack, after all, had done this kind of thing so many times before.

Consider too the taking of trophies – souvenirs taken from a body or crime scene to remind a killer of his moment of triumph - and how this impacts upon our task of profiling the murderer. A couple of brass rings were taken from Chapman's fingers, and as worthless as they may be to any other soul, they can serve one of two purposes. They are either used to prove to a third party that the act has been carried out, or they serve to allow the Ripper to psychologically and sexually revisit the crime during down time. The latter is more likely to be true. The taking of body parts which of course will decompose very quickly after their removal, is a very different story. Where does he store them? What will he do with them? Coming back home with a couple of rings can easily be explained to your missus: you found them or you won them in a game of cards, but coming back home with a bladder – now that takes some explaining. No, the removal of body parts is for him and him alone. It is like raising a flag on Everest. It signifies the ultimate victory.

And while the actual kill is over too quickly, the sexual high and the probable orgasm that he achieves during his bloodlust is in danger of being lost or tarnished with memory, then the handling of these slippery trophies can be savoured for a little while longer in the comparative safety of his own place and time.

Something else of significance that may have arisen following the murder, concerns the posters that were suddenly seen on every street corner: "Capture Leather Apron" they proclaimed, referring to the identity of the innocent and now underground Mr. Pizer. (This description comes about when a piece of bloody leather apron is found next to Chapman's body, and as local criminal John Pizer is already know by the nickname of Leather Apron, it is not a huge leap from artefact to individual.)

Consider for one moment the mind of the murderer. He has just committed an almost perfect crime. He and he alone has excited not just the Metropolis but the world. He is invincible; he wanders the streets untouched and unseen by the police, selecting his victims at will and disappearing into the ether - and the authorities call him...Leather Apron!

If we consider contemporary serial killers whose work and name has been underwhelmed or ignored by the newspapers – men like Colin Ireland for example. What do they do? They write to the press and the police and they suggest names to match their crimes. Ireland told them to call him the *Fairy Eliminator*, which advice they completely and quite properly ignored. Dennis Rader suggested dozens of names, one of which, the *BTK Killer* stuck, thereby elevating his self worth and public persona.

So what of our man's reaction when he is labeled by the almost derisory title Leather Apron? Would he not write to the "Boss" and sign his letter with a name befitting his ego and thoroughly deserved accomplishments? Was that how and why *Jack the Ripper* came about?

I would be surprised if Jack was not one of the thousands of Londoners who turned out on the streets following Chapman's murder, enjoying guided tours of the murder scene at 29 Hanbury Street. Jack, after all, was now a celebrity. He was feeding on the palpable fear that his handiwork had excited among his public. And where better to hear what his fans were saying about him than right there on the streets? One thing was for sure. Jack could not stop now.

'Liz Stride...Not how it was meant to be.

In Dianne's initial thoughts, Berner Street, the last place that Elizabeth Stride was seen alive, was a stone's throw from Whitechapel's Grove Street. It would have been very tempting to think that from Belcher's own little domicile he could have easily spat the distance between the two terraces.

That he may also have heard the shouts at eleven o' clock on the night of 29th September as two impudent workmen called out to Liz Stride, "Watch out! That's Leather Apron getting around you," was also a tempting thought. But regardless of the fact that our man lived five miles  from here, he would have known the area well from his work, and may well have been watching quietly from the shadows as he selected his next victim.

At the time in question, 11 p.m., she and a prospective customer were hugging and kissing in the doorway of the Bricklayer's Arms pub on Settle Street. The two hurried off in the direction of Berner Street, where Stride hung around for over an hour. It is this hour, the last in 44 year old Stride's troubled life that we must concern ourselves with if we are to deepen our understanding of Jack. As usual there are a number of problems standing in our way.

Official reports have long gone and it is to the daily newspapers that we have to turn for much of the information that we need to choreograph events of the 29th and 30th September 1888. Not unusually, content within the news is conflicting to say the least. It would not be a newspaper if the facts were not twisted to suit the tastes and appetite of their readership, but we must be grateful for small mercies.

Had the murderer been caught on the night that became known as the "Double Event" – (the murder of Elizabeth Stride and Catherine Eddowes) then the duty inspector would have compiled a committal file, consisting of all available witness statements. These would have been assessed for content, particularly with a view to relevance and robustness when the witness would ultimately be cross examined by counsel for the defence. (Having once witnessed a defence barrister shamefully rip apart an eight year old rape victim I know full well the standards of evidence required and the unscrupulous nature of some individuals in wigs. If a terrified child could – and still can be treated in that way, there was little hope that an adult would receive any special favours, especially back in '88.)

Those who claim to have seen and transacted with Liz Stride can really be whittled down to two reliable sources: The local bobby, Police Constable William Smith and Louis Diemshutz who discovered her body. The others have so many holes in their stories as to make them very dubious at best.

Among the most intriguing statement was that given by a Jew named Israel Shwartz who allegedly sees Stride being ill treated by one male while another pipe smoking individual, possibly acting in tandem, calls out "Lipski" before making for the terrified old chap. Lipski, being an epithet for either Jew or murder was a definite precursor to something bad happening to the man, who did not hang about to find out which version was intended.

Only the previous year, a Jew named Israel Lipski was convicted and hanged for the murder of a lady called Miriam Angel, at 22 Batty Street (which runs parallel to Berner Street.) and as anti-Semitic feelings were tangible in the area, it is understandable that Shwartz made himself scarce.

That Hungarian Shwartz spoke no English effectively meant that his statement (given when he and a friend attended the police station voluntarily the next day) was that of someone else; interpreters have to make the best of what they *think* is being said, and translate that into what they *think* it should be. Not a great combination when words like push and shove are easily confused, yet so important in their painting of an accurate picture.

The Star newspaper, having learned of Schwartz's relevance to the case, sent out a reporter who tracked him down and interviewed him for the benefit of their readers. The inconsistencies between the official and the newspaper statements, (detailed on the website Casebook.org) are as follows:

- In the police statement, the first man tries to pull Stride *from* the passage - in the second, he tries to push her *into* the passage.
- In the *Star* interview, it is the second man (not the first) who yells "a warning" (as opposed to "Lipski!" in the police statement)
- In the *Star* interview, the second man has *red moustaches* - in the police statement, there is no mention of moustaches on the second man, who is then described as having light brown hair.

Of course, the differences are minimal, but put this before a decent defence barrister and your case begins to evaporate.

From the statements taken by witnesses in the hour prior to her death, we must first consider that of William Marshall, who at 11.45 p.m. sees a woman he believes to be Stride with a male wearing a short black cutaway coat and a sailor's hat. The two are exchanging kisses and pleasantries near to Marshall's Lodging House at 64 Berner Street. Although the street lighting was pitifully gloomy in this location, Marshall describes a stout middle-aged man of around 5'6" in height and having the appearance of a clerk. He does not see the man's face clearly which makes his assessment of age a guess at very best. He would later identify Stride more by her clothing than her face, but giving him the benefit of the doubt, he may well have witnessed Elizabeth with a prospective customer.

Constable William Smith sees Stride some forty five minutes later, at around 12.35 a.m. At this time she is on Berner Street, only a short distance from the yard in which her body will soon be found. The officer has a good look at the girl and will later testify with confidence that it was Stride, whom he will also see at the dump spot and mortuary. Unfortunately he does not take much notice of the male, but sees that he is around 5'7" in height and dressed in dark clothes and hard felt deerstalker hat. Liz is wearing a flower pinned to her jacket breast and the male carries a newspaper parcel, measuring 18" by 6".

It is significant that at this time Stride will undoubtedly have seen the officer and would, if she felt in any way threatened by the male, have called out for help. She is obviously comfortable in his presence. Likewise, it is safe to assume that the male will be cognisant of the officer's steady perambulations as his "heavy tramp" can be heard by another witness from within her house at the same time. This being the case, our chap will know that he has a window of around twenty five to thirty minutes before the constable will revisit that spot on the regular circumnavigation of his beat. We have already learned that Jack would find thirty minutes an ample timeframe in which to carry out his operation. To deliberately wait for such a passing is risky but calculatingly clever.

Louis Diemshutz was the steward of a club that opened into Dutfield's Yard, a gated alley that ran off Berner Street. At 1 a.m. he returned from a trip to market, riding a costermonger's barrow which was pulled by a pony. Having turned into the yard, the gates of which were not unusually open, the pony immediately shied away from some object to its right. From the back of the barrow Diemshutz peered into the blackness to see what it was that caused the beast to be spooked so, but being unable to discern more than a black shape against the wall, he jumped down and struck a match. He could just make out the shape of a woman and not wishing to investigate alone, he ran into the club to garner assistance. The poor man's first thought was that the body may have been his "missus", and after ascertaining that she was indeed well, he returned to the alley with a young club-goer, a tailor named Kozebrodski. The two men, armed with a candle took a cursory look at the corpse and ran off without disturbing it, shouting for the police. They ran as far as Grove Street, in order to secure the attendance of a lawman.

At the same time, another club-goer, a Russian named Morris Eagle, sought to pay the dead Ms Stride a visit, scaring himself witless by the sight of the blood running from the woman's throat. It was he who managed to summon a police constable, P.C. Lamb, whom he found up on Commercial Road.

By 1.15 a.m. Doctor Blackwell was at the scene, carrying out a remarkably detailed examination of Stride's body - bearing in mind that the only light that was available was the dull glow of a policeman's bulls-eye lamp. By this time however, our man had disappeared into the night.

Whoever carried out the murder had obviously been disturbed by Diemshutz, otherwise the victim would have suffered the same fate as those previous. All he had on this occasion managed to achieve, was the slicing of her throat and this, enough to silence and kill her, was far from the desired objective. It is likely that the Ripper was hiding in the shadows, cursing his bad luck as Diemshutz rode into the yard; he would have waited only long enough to see the terrified costermonger run into the club before making his own exit out into Berner Street and off in search of a second victim.

Here the Ripper needed to use all of his uncanny skills of survival. He knew that once the first policeman's whistles shrilled out in the night, then every bobby in a square mile would be running to Berner Street for a piece of the action. If, like William Belcher, you were savvy to the streets and the likely actions of the police, then your next move may have been predetermined in that just-in-case world of the organised killer.

First thought would be with the nearest lawman – Constable Smith - whom you had just a few minutes earlier heard tramping past you and your intended victim, and whose beat took in the terraces at Grove Street. Run in that direction and you run into the arms of the Old Bill. That would be plain silly. The direction in which you must flee is the opposite – west. And to make it even harder for the boys in blue to buckle you, cross over the Whitechapel Road and slip quietly into Mitre Square. Here, less than a mile away would lie sanctuary courtesy of the City of London Police.

The gulf between the two manors policed by the City and the Metropolitan boys was enormous. (It was equivalent to crossing the State Line over in the U.S., an imaginary Iron Curtain that divided a city. In America the FBI might chip in and bridge the divide with expertise to help solve your case, but here there existed a professional jealousy that was historically nigh on impossible to breach.)

Catching your breath in the shadows of Church Passage with adrenalin coursing through your veins and the sting of sexual arousal still playing out its overtures deep within – you had cunningly bought yourself time: All you had to do now was wait. Your next pretty lady is almost upon you.

Catherine Eddowes, the Ripper's next victim, was 46 years of age when she met her untimely death. She was born in Wolverhampton and finally migrated to the capital in 1881. In common with many of the prostitutes in Whitechapel, Catherine, mother to three children, was separated from her  life partner and was prone to drinking heavily. Described as an intelligent, scholarly woman, she was possessed of a foul temper, yet the statements made by the officers in whose custody she found herself on Saturday September 29th, tell of a woman with a friendly, if not impish disposition.

By the time that the crowds had gathered in Dutfield's Yard, Catherine Eddowes was already on a collision course with death. Her evening had begun in blissful ignorance and drunken insensibility, flat out on the wet pavements up on Aldgate High Street. The officer who came upon the unfortunate prostitute and whose fruitless attempts to raise the woman up to a vertical position would later be well placed to identify her corpse at the mortuary. For now however, he and another officer busied themselves with raising Catherine to her feet and hauling her back to Bishopsgate Police Station. There she was housed in a drunk cell with its low bench bed to prevent injury by falling and a drain in the floor to accommodate vomit and other diverse excretions. Here she would remain until at 12.55 a.m. Police Sergeant Byfield deemed that she was sober enough to be released. She gave her name as Mary Ann Kelly and after exchanging good natured impudence with Police Constable Hutt she emerged once more into the night air.

Eddowes now had a choice to make. Should she turn right and head home to Flower and Dean Street, or should she head off in some other direction and seek a few pennies for drink – and possibly her bed for the night – courtesy of whichever gentleman she may come upon on her meanderings. She chose option two, and unwittingly set sail on a course that would lead her into the arms of a man who entertained more than thoughts of a loving embrace.

At around 1.35 a.m. three local men left the Imperial Club in Duke Street, at the corner of which lay Church Passage. They saw there a woman whom it was believed was Eddowes chatting amiably to a man. Her hand was placed on the man's chest in what was translated as no more than friendly and tactile contact and which was probably part of Eddowes' encouraging sales pitch, or pre sex negotiations. One of those men, commercial traveller Joseph Lawende would later identify the clothes that Eddowes was wearing and which were removed from her corpse.

The man, described to police as around 30 years of age, medium build, 5 feet 7 inches tall, fair complexion and a moustache. He is wearing a pepper and salt coloured jacket which fits loosely, a grey cloth cap with a peak of the same colour. He has a reddish handkerchief knotted around his neck. Over all he gives the appearance of being a sailor.

Nothing in the demeanor of either Catherine or her gentleman friend gives the three professional chaps any cause for concern, further reinforcing the smooth and confident style employed by the murderer and this despite what must have been a heart stopping few minutes earlier back in Dutfield's Yard.

Around fifteen minutes after Joseph Lawende sees Eddowes and her punter, Police Constable Edward Watkins discovered her body in Mitre Square. In less than a quarter of an hour the killer had slit her throat and carried out not just the removal of womb and left kidney, but also mutilated her face in a final dehumanising act.

The officer would run off in a frantic bid to summon assistance and within a very short time had secured the attendance of senior officers, together with Dr. Frederick Gordon Brown, a City of London Police Surgeon. He would later state:

"The body was on its back, the head turned to left shoulder. The arms by the side of the body as if they had fallen there. Both palms upwards, the fingers slightly bent. The left leg extended in a line with the body. The abdomen was exposed. Right leg bent at the thigh and knee. The throat cut across.

The intestines were drawn out to a large extent and placed over the right shoulder; they were smeared over with some feculent matter. A piece of about two feet was quite detached from the body and placed between the body and the left arm, apparently by design. The lobe and auricle of the right ear were cut obliquely through.

There was a quantity of clotted blood on the pavement on the left side of the neck round the shoulder and upper part of arm, and fluid blood-coloured serum which had flowed under the neck to the right shoulder, the pavement sloping in that direction.

Body was quite warm. No death stiffening had taken place. She must have been dead most likely within the half hour. We looked for superficial bruises and saw none. No blood on the skin of the abdomen or secretion of any kind on the thighs. No spurting of blood on the bricks or pavement around. No marks of blood below the middle of the body. Several buttons were found in the clotted blood after the body was removed. There was no blood on the front of the clothes. There were no traces of recent connexion. (Sexual intercourse.)

When the body arrived at Golden Lane, some of the blood was dispersed through the removal of the body to the mortuary. The clothes were taken off carefully from the body. A piece of deceased's ear dropped from the clothing.

I made a post mortem examination at half past two on Sunday afternoon. Rigor mortis was well marked; body not quite cold. Green discolouration over the abdomen.

After washing the left hand carefully, a bruise the size of a sixpence, recent and red, was discovered on the back of the left hand between the thumb and first finger. A few small bruises on right shin of older date. The hands and arms were bronzed. No bruises on the scalp, the back of the body, or the elbows.

The face was very much mutilated. There was a cut about a quarter of an inch through the lower left eyelid, dividing the structures completely through the upper eyelid on that side. There was a scratch through the skin on the left upper eyelid - near to the angle of the nose. The right eyelid was cut through to about half an inch.

There was a deep cut over the bridge of the nose, extending from the left border of the nasal bone down near the angle of the jaw on the right side of the cheek. This cut went into the bone and divided all the structures of the cheek except the mucous membrane of the mouth.

The tip of the nose was quite detached by an oblique cut from the bottom of the nasal bone to where the wings of the nose join on to the face. A cut from this divided the upper lip and extended through the substance of the gum over the right upper lateral incisor tooth.

About half an inch from the top of the nose was another oblique cut. There was a cut on the right angle of the mouth as if the cut of a point of a knife. The cut extended an inch and a half, parallel with the lower lip.

There was on each side of her cheek a cut which peeled up the skin, forming a triangular flap about an inch and a half. On the left cheek there were two abrasions of the epithelium under the left ear.

The throat was cut across to the extent of about six or seven inches. A superficial cut commenced about an inch and a half below the lobe, and about two and a half inches behind the left ear, and extended across the throat to about three inches below the lobe of the right ear.

The big muscle across the throat was divided through on the left side. The large vessels on the left side of the neck were severed. The larynx was severed below the vocal cord. All the deep structures were severed to the bone, the knife marking intervertebral cartilages. The sheath of the vessels on the right side was just opened.

The carotid artery had a fine hole opening, the internal jugular vein was opened about an inch and a half -- not divided. The blood vessels contained clot. All these injuries were performed by a sharp instrument like a knife, and pointed.

The cause of death was haemorrhage from the left common carotid artery. The death was immediate and the mutilations were inflicted after death.

We examined the abdomen. The front walls were laid open from the breast bones to the pubes. The cut commenced opposite the ensiform cartilage. The incision went upwards, not penetrating the skin that was over the sternum. It then divided the ensiform cartilage. The knife must have cut obliquely at the expense of that cartilage.

Behind this, the liver was stabbed as if by the point of a sharp instrument. Below this was another incision into the liver of about two and a half inches, and below this the left lobe of the liver was slit through by a vertical cut. Two cuts were shewn by a jagging of the skin on the left side.

The abdominal walls were divided in the middle line to within a quarter of an inch of the navel. The cut then took a horizontal course for two inches and a half towards the right side. It then divided round the navel on the left side, and made a parallel incision to the former horizontal incision, leaving the navel on a tongue of skin. Attached to the navel was two and a half inches of the lower part of the rectus muscle on the left side of the abdomen. The incision then took an oblique direction to the right and was shelving. The incision went down the right side of the vagina and rectum for half an inch behind the rectum.

There was a stab of about an inch on the left groin. This was done by a pointed instrument. Below this was a cut of three inches going through all tissues making a wound of the peritoneum about the same extent.

An inch below the crease of the thigh was a cut extending from the anterior spine of the ilium obliquely down the inner side of the left thigh and separating the left labium, forming a flap of skin up to the groin. The left rectus muscle was not detached.

There was a flap of skin formed by the right thigh, attaching the right labium, and extending up to the spine of the ilium. The muscles on the right side inserted into the frontal ligaments were cut through.

The skin was retracted through the whole of the cut through the abdomen, but the vessels were not clotted. Nor had there been any appreciable bleeding from the vessels. I draw the conclusion that the act was made after death, and there would not have been much blood on the murderer. The cut was made by someone on the right side of the body, kneeling below the middle of the body.

I removed the content of the stomach and placed it in a jar for further examination. There seemed very little in it in the way of food or fluid, but from the cut end partly digested farinaceous food escaped.

The intestines had been detached to a large extent from the mesentery. About two feet of the colon was cut away. The sigmoid flexure was invaginated into the rectum very tightly.

Right kidney was pale, bloodless with slight congestion of the base of the pyramids.

There was a cut from the upper part of the slit on the under surface of the liver to the left side, and another cut at right angles to this, which were about an inch and a half deep and two and a half inches long. Liver itself was healthy.

The gall bladder contained bile. The pancreas was cut, but not through, on the left side of the spinal column. Three and a half inches of the lower border of the spleen (by half an inch) was attached to the peritoneum.

The peritoneal lining was cut through on the left side and the left kidney carefully taken out and removed. The left renal artery was cut through. I would say that someone who knew the position of the kidney must have done it.

The lining membrane over the uterus was cut through. The womb was cut through horizontally, leaving a stump of three quarters of an inch. The rest of the womb had been taken away with some of the ligaments. The vagina and cervix of the womb was uninjured.

The bladder was healthy and uninjured, and contained three or four ounces of water. There was a tongue-like cut through the anterior wall of the abdominal aorta. The other organs were healthy. There were no indications of connexion.

I believe the wound in the throat was first inflicted. I believe she must have been lying on the ground.

The wounds on the face and abdomen prove that they were inflicted by a sharp, pointed knife, and that in the abdomen by one six inches or longer.

I believe the perpetrator of the act must have had considerable knowledge of the position of the organs in the abdominal cavity and the way of removing them. It required a great deal of medical knowledge to have removed the kidney and to know where it was placed. The parts removed would be of no use for any professional purpose.

I think the perpetrator of this act had sufficient time, or he would not have nicked the lower eyelids. It would take at least five minutes.

I cannot assign any reason for the parts being taken away. I feel sure that there was no struggle, and believe it was the act of one person.

The throat had been so instantly severed that no noise could have been emitted. I should not expect much blood to have been found on the person who had inflicted these wounds. The wounds could not have been self-inflicted.

My attention was called to the apron, (*that she was wearing at the time of her murder, a piece of which was found at nearby Goulston Street.*) particularly the corner of the apron with a string attached. The blood spots were of recent origin. I have seen the portion of an apron produced by Dr. Phillips and stated to have been found in Goulston Street. It is impossible to say that it is human blood on the apron. I fitted the piece of apron, which had a new piece of material on it (which had evidently been sewn on to the piece I have), the seams of the two actually corresponding. Some blood and apparently faecal matter was found on the portion that was found in Goulston Street."

Whoever murdered these girls and indeed whichever direction he travelled, this escape route would have been a major consideration before and during the commission of his crimes. And even though the execution of Eddowes was not part of the initial plan, his post offence activity was carried out with devastating effectiveness.

Like everything else that he seemed to do, despite the massive risk of being caught, his modus operandi seemed to incorporate an excellent system for slipping silently away following his crimes.

Much has been made of the reason that the killer took the piece of apron and why he left it in the place that he did, outside of an establishment that was known to be frequented by Jews. Police Constable Alf Long who found the small piece of material and of course the famous and contentious graffiti, inferring that the Jews will be blamed for nothing (the accurate wording has long been disputed), had no idea that there had been a murder a few streets away, when at around 2.55 a.m. he came upon the material upon the ground.

It seems unusual that the officer would pay the slightest attention to a piece of rag lying in a street that would probably have been littered with all manner of rubbish anyway, but accept his evidence we must, speculating instead on the reason that the killer would leave it and the graffiti here. (P.C. Long is sure that the graffiti was not there on the last perambulation of his beat).

Perhaps, having been disturbed twice in the matter of Elizabeth Stride by Jews – Schwartz and Diemeshutz, he sought to exact a bit of revenge by leaving defamatory remarks and evidence from the murder outside of a Jewish establishment. Perhaps the material and the graffiti were attributable to separate individuals. Frustratingly this is yet another area that will never be known.

And then one must ask why the killer carried that piece of rag all the way to Goulston Street before throwing it away. Did he use it to wipe his weapon – or would this have been discarded much nearer to Mitre Square? Did he use it to wrap and carry the kidney in – in which case why did he discard it here in the street instead of carrying it to his destination? Tiny anomalies like these are what make this case so fascinating.

Perhaps we should also consider, as I am sure he himself did - the likelihood of being disturbed during a murder. What would he do? With a six inch knife, sharpened like a cutthroat razor, it would have taken an exceptional human being to stop him. By the time that the Ripper's felonious activities had registered in the mind of any potential witness, he or she would have been clutching at a throat that was gaping wide open and hanging on grimly to a life that was already slipping away. Louis Diemshutz was a very lucky man indeed!

Squeezing the trigger

And so, as dawn broke on 30th September 1888, two of the two finest police forces in the world were running into blind alleys and clutching at shadows. Their attempts to capture the author of this dreadful series of murders had failed miserably. They had neither the man nor the weapon used to slit the throats of the corpses who were now reposing in their various places of rest. As detectives sniffed at the smoking gun they must have longed for a chance to see the man who had pulled the trigger and who was leading them such a merry dance.

In a case such as this, carried out at a time when medical and other records often did not exist, it is only in the exceptional circumstance that we can find out what went on in someone's head; what changed a normal human being and turned him into a lethal killer. Indeed we have the smoking gun, but what, when and who actually pulled that trigger?

If William Belcher can truly be considered to be a candidate for murder, then we need to take a close look at his inner workings; find out what changed a child full of wonder and joy for this world into a young man so full of hatred and bitterness that he may have set out on a journey that left crumpled bodies in its wake. We are indeed fortunate in this respect, for documents that Dianne uncovered help us to piece together life during a five year period in the family home at 20 Grove Street, Whitechapel.

The property was a typical London terrace, tenemented and rented out, room by room, to working families of the lower classes. The 1881 census shows us that there were twenty persons living in the house, the Belchers being the largest of five families spread out over two floors.

We know that Benjamin Belcher, the lad's father, slipped in and out of Marylebone like a roving merchantmen, stopping only long enough to show his face before disappearing once more into the ether. Mother Ellen, through desperation or entertainment, we know not which, had already served six months imprisonment for thievery when young William was only three years of age. This fact tells us quite clearly that she is capable of drifting into unlawful activities should the need or whim arise.

Following her release in 1868, there appeared to be no recidivistic tendencies and Grove Street may have echoed with something resembling normality for another seven years. In 1875 however, all that was to change.

William was ten years of age when his mother showed the first signs of illness. Constant coughing and breathlessness were something that Londoners were well used to, breathing in the vitiated air of a city that spewed out toxins and sulphurous fumes from every chimney, but this was different. The bloody phlegm and the chronic fatigue were a precursor to a disease that spelled almost certain death: Consumption.

For the poor folk of London and every other town and city, consumption, or tuberculosis as we now call it, was fatal in over eighty percent of cases. Doctors would have treated the patients for coughs or the pain that came with the disease, but little relief could be obtained by physicians or street corner cure-all remedies.

The best treatment available would come in the sanatoriums where patients could breathe in clean seaside or mountain air; for Ellen Belcher this was no more than an impossible dream. For her it was the damp of winter and the smog of still summer nights. For her it was lungs that rattled and sleepless nights and a body that grew weaker by the day.

As Ellen struggled to bring up her three sons, the youngest, Frederick being just four years old, daily chores would fall more and more on the shoulders of William. Father of course was permanently absent, and could no longer be relied upon to provide any financial or other support. And while William could lift and carry and run the odd errand, someone had to earn the money to provide sustenance, clothe the lads and pay the rent. That someone, regardless of her physical deterioration, was Ellen Belcher.

We must be careful not to tar our matriarch with a very dirty brush here, but two factors point towards the fact that Ellen may have turned to life on the streets – or indeed life on the mattress in her fetid kitchen at 20 Grove Street – in order that she and her brood could survive.

Fact number one: survive she did.

Fact number two: without a husband, and with no known means of support or gentlemanly cohabitation, Ellen Belcher gave birth to three children, one after the other, before her life finally expired. 1877 saw the birth of Joseph, followed next year by Ellen and then Annie in 1879. Compared to the children who had gone before, in happier times perhaps, or indeed more socially acceptable times - these last three children were never formally registered and we have to rely on the census for

	Registration District	St. Marylebone				
DEATHS in the Sub-District of ... in the County of ...						
When and Where Died	Name and Surname	Sex.	Age.	Rank or Profession.	Cause of Death.	Signature, Description, and Residence of Informant.
Twenty seventh April 1880 20 Grove Street	Ellen Belcher	Female	37 years	Wife of Benjamin Belcher House painter	Premature labour (6 months) Flooding and exhaustion 14 days Phthisis 5 years certified by Bullock MRCS	M Reed present at the death 20 Grove Street Marylebone

our information. (This was to be a pattern in omission that the Belchers seemed to follow both here and later in Hartlepool. No record means no existence.)

And even then, with six youngsters and still hanging on to life by a thread, Ellen Belcher must have been unable to rest her weary bones. By October 1879, she was pregnant again. This time however, the unborn child would suck the last ounce of life from its dying mother; on 27th April 1880, Ellen Belcher went into premature labour, haemorrhaging violently, unable to summon the strength to abort the foetus within. Before the day was over, she and her unborn child were dead. Fifteen year old William had seen the slow and undignified demise of his own mother. He had watched her through pregnancy after pregnancy and each child that was brought into the world would be another burden on his young shoulders. Had Ellen indeed entertained a queue of eager and fumbling men while her children slept fitfully around her, then William Belcher may have understandably developed an extreme hatred of prostitution and the social paraphernalia that went with it.

And now his mother lay dead; inside of her womb was that parasite that had brought about her end. How he would have loved to rip that which had caused so much misery and death out of her insides. But it was all up to him now - she had left him in charge of her brood: Three little girls and three younger brothers. Whatever brief snatch at childhood William Benjamin Belcher may have enjoyed, it was now long behind him. Seven years later, in 1887, something else would happen that would not only reopen old wounds, but would also make the Belcher name an object of derision and hatred. And once again, those ladies of the night lay at the heart of all things destructive.

On the Street where you live

When Dianne first presented her evidence for my perusal, the location of the Belcher's domicile, Grove Street, Whitechapel, seemed to be unchallengeable. Slap bang in the middle of the action, and only two streets away from Berner Street, it certainly seemed to put William on the doorstep for murder. And no matter how deep she searched for locus confirmation, being no Londoner, she ended up at the same place.

I did initially feel uneasy with this location, for one or two solid reasons. Primarily, the murder of Stride, two streets away from home, was a little bit too close for comfort, and if he had indeed lived here for some time, he would be well known to all and sundry – perhaps a little too well known. Although Jack was engaged in a high risk business, even this degree of exposure seemed a step too far. To be seen chatting to Stride and soliciting her attentions so openly would definitely be asking for trouble. And trouble in this case meant the hanging variety.

Secondly, a serial killer who had reached the zenith of his fantasy-driven career, which with Nichols and Chapman would certainly seem to be the case, must surely have started that career in an albeit slightly less barbarous way closer to home.

The seven mile rule applies here, and one would assume that experimental killings or petty crime would have been committed close by before he branched out to a safer location and one in which he was less well known.

Nevertheless, I had to present findings based on the information given, and did so with Grove Street Whitechapel in mind. Things were about to change however, with the publication of our first print run.

Once in the public eye and with the inevitable scrutiny that the work would come under, an email arrived from a self-styled Ripperologist of good pedigree, who pointed out through her extensive knowledge of the Metropolis, that there was in fact another Grove Street, this forming part of Lisson Grove in neighbouring Marylebone.

There was no hiding from this fact and I duly informed Dianne that an error had been made. Perhaps even a fatal error when it came to the question of Belcher being The Ripper. If this new Grove Street were too far away from the epicentre of Jack's ultimate killing ground, then it was game over.

Dianne returned to the drawing board a little less disappointed than I, delivering soon after yet another batch of information. It was time to review what we already had and where this new information fitted.

Grove Street mark two was indeed in Marylebone, but more importantly, the estimated walking distance between this one and Whitechapel High Street was just under five miles. One could walk this in a very short time, or take the tube in an even shorter time!

This was indeed good news, and if activity fitting a serial killer's early years could be found in the vicinity, then our seven mile rule was looking particularly good.

The first step, in order to acquaint myself and our non-London readers with a picture of this new Belcher residence, was to draw upon contemporary sources to paint as clear a picture as is possible of Grove Street mark two. As an artist I enjoy using colours to paint any picture that sits upon my easel. This picture would need only one tube from my paint box. Black.

To say that this part of town was the pits would probably have increased property values by fifty percent. This was in fact one of the capital's worst slums, notorious for drinking, crime and prostitution. Its poorest residents lived in squalor in the once grand, but now crumbling old terraces. Contemporary sources tell us that bobbies patrolled in pairs in order that they may be afforded some safety and that the women of the area were "the most drunken, violent and foul-mouthed in all London". To compound matters, gangs roamed the streets terrorising locals of a delicate nature and no doubt tightly controlling the prostitutes who worked herein.

Here in 1885, thirteen year old Eliza Armstrong was sold to a brothel keeper for five pounds and the resulting publicity not only changed the age of consent but made the name of Marylebone synonymous with filth and vice.

All in all, the Belchers couldn't have chosen a less savoury place in which to bring up their children, even if they had tried. Their own crumbling manse at number 20 Grove Street had long been reduced to a series of rented rooms with five families and twenty souls paying a few shillings a week for the privilege of having a roof over their heads.

Heads of households, or to be more precise, the breadwinners in each room, consisted of the lowest menial workers. A gas fitter, a stationers assistant, a joiner and porter, and of course a milk carrier, all brought back their meagre wages in order that they and their families might survive.

Downstairs at the back of the house, the Belchers and their lodger, all nine of them, did not even have the luxury of a space that they could call a living room in which to dwell. In an unfurnished kitchen with neither sanitation nor space to breathe, the clan struggled with daily chores, eating, sleeping and carrying out their ablutions, in a space that would strip any human being of every last shred of dignity that they once possessed.

That poor Ellen Belcher gave birth to a succession of tiny souls and eventually died with the rattle of TB on her lungs in this squalid environment beggars modern understanding. That she may well, like many of her contemporaries, have also carried on a trade as a prostitute within these same four walls paints a darker picture than could ever be represented on canvas, whether executed by Walter Sickert or any other who knew the locale and had a penchant for the graphic capture of such depravation.

And of course, having finally placed young William here, we must look around the immediate streets and seek out a murder or two that may have been forerunners to the grand prix of carnage that lay ahead. Perhaps a crime that would show that our lad had acquired a taste for the slicing of throats and that butchery, even of his fellow human beings, would be no bar to a chap with his not-so-delicate sensibilities.

Thus, allow me to lead you from the Belcher's kitchen-room, down the hall and out to the front door of 20 Grove Street. Turn right as you leave and drop down towards the river. Crossing over the main road into Seymour Place you will arrive at your destination in around five minutes.

The place is George Street. The time is 8 p.m. on Saturday 21st January 1888. The subject of our initial observations is a well-dressed young man who is hammering on the door of number 86.

Francis Clark bears a letter for his 49 year old sister Lucy. He is anxious that he might invite Lucy for dinner; he also wishes to discuss a family matter and seek his sister's advice. Receiving no reply, he waits for around three quarters of an hour before giving up and sliding a hastily written note under the door and heading off from whence he came. What he does not know is that Lucy is indeed home, but that she is quite incapable of answering his calls. Lucy has been dead for around twenty four hours and her body will lay a while longer before it is eventually discovered.

Lucy Clark was a successful dressmaker, (that being one who does indeed fashion fine garments and not a euphemism for a lower form of occupation). She was, following a profitable period of self-employment, possessed of means and the outward signs of moderate wealth. These things would not have gone unnoticed by the covetous eyes of those up at Lisson Grove.

86 George Street probably displayed a "To Let" sign outside, for the premises were indeed being offered for rent, that being with the exception of the second floor wherein Lucy herself lived.

We know that Lucy was alive on the Friday afternoon prior to her brother's visit, as she was seen in nearby Baker Street by a neighbour and others who ran businesses in Marylebone. Her disposition according to witnesses was cheerful, this seeming to rule out suicide in the eyes of the reporting newspapers.

On the evening of Monday 23rd January, William Betts, the letting agent, visited 86 George Street in the company of two women, in order that they might view the unoccupied part of the house. To facilitate their viewing he entered via the shop which formed the ground floor, and walked up the passage towards the rear of the building. It was there, at the bottom of the stairs, that he saw the body of Lucy Clark.

Ushering out the prospective renters, Betts ran out into the street in order to summon a constable, which some minutes later he did. Constable James Grayston accompanied Betts to the premises and being now quite dark, illuminated the scene with a match. He took hold of Lucy's hand and found it to be "cold and stiff", announcing hereafter, "Oh yes, she is dead."

Had Lucy's arm been stiff with rigor, then it is likely that she had been dead for some time. (Following the rigid state of rigor mortis, the body will, through decomposition, return to and remain in a flaccid condition. It is very likely that the house was extremely cold and this would lengthen the period in which rigor would commence and remain.)

The constable then, in accordance with his Standing Orders, is required to secure the attendance of a medical man. He runs to nearby streets and after several abortive attempts, eventually finds a doctor at home. Dr. Henry Times then begins his own examination of the crime scene.

Lucy had been dead for several days; the appearance of her body and the state of decomposition would pinpoint the rough time of death to Friday evening which was, coincidentally the Ripper's favourite night for killing.

Ms Clark's skull had been fractured and her throat had been cut, the wound reaching her vertebrae, thus indicating the strength of her assailant and the sharpness of the weapon used.

Lucy's skirts were found to be in disarray, but whether from a sexual assault, a struggle or from her body falling we cannot be certain. What is for sure is that the rooms in which she dwelt had been thoroughly ransacked and certain items of property had been removed.

In the following days and weeks the local newspapers made much of the case, reporting every rumour and release of evidence that could lay their hands upon. Police arrested Ms Clark's nephews with whom she had recently quarrelled and eventually released them without charge.

And, despite the fact that a strange young man had some weeks earlier been seen to either stalk or carry out extensive observations on the victim, the case of Ms Lucy Clark would soon be forgotten. After all, waiting in the wings was a scoop so big that it would consume the press for a century and a quarter to come.

Of course, it would border on crass to pin this murder on an embryonic Jack; a serial killer learning his trade and breaking out from the pupa that restricts him to crude acquisitional crimes where murder is a means to an end. It would be crass but it would also be foolish to rule him out.

If our chap does indeed emigrate from Marylebone's too-close-for-comfort shackles and heads off for pastures anew a few miles down the road, would his interim crimes include Spitalfield's Annie Millwood on February 25, 1888, stabbed about the lower body and eventually dying from unrelated complications? Could Ada Wilson have followed some weeks later, On March 28, 1888? Home alone at 19 Maidman Street, Wilson answered a knock at the door to find a man of about 30 years of age, 5ft 6ins in height, with a sunburnt face and a fair moustache. He was wearing a dark coat, light trousers and a wide-awake hat. The man forced his way into the room and demanded money, and when she refused he stabbed her twice in the throat and ran, leaving her for dead.

Like Lucy Clark, Wilson, although considerably poorer, was likely to be a robbery gone wrong. But once again, as we creep ever nearer Smith, Tabram and Nichols, this is ideal training ground for a young Jack. No investigating police officer in his right mind, regardless of the differences in modus operandi, would rule out this string of crimes without due consideration and good reason. After all, the perpetrator demonstrates in each case a propensity for stabbing and slicing; a merciless disposition and a driving force that allows no human to stand in his way.

We know of course what happened next and who would use those qualities to devastating effect.

It may also be worthy of mention that on the 9th November 1888 – another Friday night, a Dear Boss letter was posted in the pillar-box at the corner of

Northumberland Street, Marylebone Road. The letter was directed to the police, and its contents were as follows:- "Dear Boss, I shall be busy to-morrow night in Marylebone-road. I have two booked for blood. Yours, Jack the Ripper. Look out about two o'clock in Marylebone-road."

That being the night that Mary Kelly would perish a few miles away, and the post box being within spitting distance from the Belcher's residence, one wonders if William was enjoying jolly japes on route to Miller's Court.

Belcher: A name to be forgotten.

During May and June of 1887, Richard Stephens, a Rescue Officer from the Charing Cross Reformatory and Refuge Union, a charitable body whose raison d'etre was to clean up the streets of all things morally injurious to children, was well entrenched and deep in observations on certain dwellings near the Walworth and Kent Roads, Southwark.

Needless to say, the premises in question were brothels, and if his log of activities was correct, they were busy ones too. Most disturbing of all, children ranging from around ten to seemingly young teenagers were particularly numerous in and around the target premises. One teenage girl in particular seemed to be incredibly active in Fagin-like procurement, securing the attendance and service of others for sexual activity. For six long weeks Stephens jotted down comings and goings prior to breaking cover and kidnapping one of the unsuspecting urchins who was just leaving the brothel with a pocket of ill-gotten pennies.

Ten year old Maria Donovan was questioned by the Rescue Officer and thereafter taken to the local nick, where she was further grilled and then detained while the officer went back in search of more young suspects. This time he claimed two more scalps, Ada Coleman, 13 and his little Fagan, Esther Belcher who was also only 13 years of age.

The officer, and of course, local detectives, now had a trio of waifs to question about activities in Rodney Place and other brothels in nearby Union Place. Before warrants could be obtained to execute upon the adult offenders, those in custody would be squeezed of every last morsel of information. What came out of those young mouths was so shocking that the public would never be exposed to its basest cache of facts. Esther Belcher though, despite her tender years, would not come out of this fiasco smelling of anything remotely rose-like. Ada Coleman would see to that.

Ada, since the death of her mother, lived with her cabman father in nearby Nelson Court. It is likely that the girl would have been left to God and good (or bad as the case turned out) neighbours. Indeed that was the case when she met up with Esther sometime in April that year. The two were known to each other, but when 16 year old Jane Bruce showed up, either by chance or arrangement, it was clear that it was only Esther who knew the older girl.

"Are you on the streets?" Esther asked of Coleman. The latter professed not to know what the

115

euphemism meant, whereby Belcher explained about the monetary benefits of this thing called prostitution. Back in the brothels in Union Place there were rooms, she told her, where men were brought to you for the purpose of sexual activity. Easy money indeed.

Coleman bemoaned the fact that she would, being an outsider, not be allowed into these rooms. Belcher assured her that if *she* was with her, then entrance – and employment was a guaranteed outcome. The three then went to a brothel at 8 Union Place to complete introductions and thereby secure a new recruit to the Game.

Mary Ann Bennett was the 34 year old madam who, it seems had the responsibility of vetting the potential of new recruits. When Coleman was brought into the parlour the youngster noticed that there were lots of men there. Belcher negotiated Colman's admission, despite the fact that the latter was concerned about getting into "a row". (Presumably she meant with her father.) Bennett assured her that this was not the case as she had no mother. (Not that this makes a great deal of sense.) She was then taken to a room by Belcher, who was obviously very well versed in these proceedings, and left alone until the arrival of a particular gentleman customer some minutes later.

Ada Coleman earned five shillings, courtesy of this punter, for her first experience of sexual service. It was, she later said, Esther Belcher who had gone outside to solicit the aforementioned gentleman for these immoral purposes. She would testify that Belcher could often be observed acting as procurer and usher, earning herself a healthy purse for these services on behalf of the madam and her entourage.

Esther Belcher's own story, particularly as it pertained to her initiation into prostitution, would later make headlines both here and abroad. She then resided at Rodney Place, just off the Kent Road, with her mother Sophia, and would have seen how active the brothels in this part of town were, eventually being secured by Jane Bruce to join the sisterhood at 8 Union Place. Belcher worked here, using rooms rented from Mary Ann Bennett, for some time, acting as a child prostitute and no doubt learning the ropes and the scams – and earning good money in the process.

But, for reasons not stated in any testament, Bennett decided that Esther Belcher could no longer use the rooms, announcing this fact when, inconveniently, the teenaged prostitute had a gentleman client in tow. Esther was taken by a man named "Tec", to another brothel in nearby Ash Street, where she paid the occupant, nineteen year old Esther Procknell for a room and belatedly entertained her client. This venue would be used regularly thereafter by Esther Belcher, who it would seem, then swung between securing youngsters for the brothels and also prostituting herself. Mary Anne Bennett obviously kept her place exclusively for older regular prostitutes and of course the brand new girls, for whose virginity a handsome price could be secured.

When Esther's mother Sophia was interviewed by the police, she admitted that her daughter "stayed out of a night until sometimes ten o'clock," adding, "there is no reason for her being out so late."

She also said that Mary Ann Bennett had on one occasion come hammering at her door – the couple were obviously known to each other – and said, "they are looking for Esther," presumably meaning the authorities. When it was explained that the reason for her being sought was that she was on the streets, Sophia seems to have shrugged her shoulders and said, "she is old enough to know better."

In a strange additional statement, which may indicate that Sophia Belcher knew full well what her daughter was about, she declared that Esther sometimes gave her ninepence or tenpence, claiming that she had earned it cleaning doorsteps.

The workhouse doctor would later examine the girls, including Belcher and certify that they had indeed lost their virginity and that their stories were true. Whether they were diseased through their activities was never disclosed.

In due course, a whole posse of adult prostitutes and pimps were brought up for trial, including Belcher, who was charged with associating with the girls. At Lambeth Police Court, Mr. Chance, chairing the first hearing, said that he could scarcely have believed that such proceedings would be carried on in a civilised society. The more sensitive ingredients of this case would never make the broadsheets or jury, making the case even more compelling for the public in the absence of these facts.

The instigators received hefty sentences, but it seems that Esther Belcher may have escaped imprisonment by the skin of her teeth, as records of her punishment cannot be traced. Regardless of that fact, public exposure via local and national newspapers, including Illustrated Police News and the Pall Mall Gazette, would ensure that the name of Belcher was so well known, that anyone bearing this identity would be immediately associated with activities in Union Place and its surrounds. William Benjamin Belcher could now have even more reason to hate prostitutes and indeed the young cousin who had brought about this stigmatic event.

What happened to her is lost to the mists of time, but we have a good idea what became of cousin William.

Only a violet from mother's grave.

From the windows of his employers, Messrs Bayle and Wright's, William Belcher could look out onto Dorset Street and watch the world drift – or stagger by, depending upon the degree of inebriation involved; the down and outs and the lads from Commercial Street Chambers for Men; the warehousemen from nearby industrial premises and of course the prostitutes across at Miller's Court. (pictured)

Miller's Court was approached from Dorset St. via a flagged passage that ran under an arch. Little more than three feet wide, it was about twenty feet long. The door to Room 13, where Mary Jane Kelly lived, was the last on the right before the passage opened out into a yard about fifteen feet square. This yard contained a water tap, a privy and a brick-built dustbin.

Mary Jane Kelly was not like the rest. At 25, she was considerably younger; at five feet seven inches she was taller and by all accounts, with youth on her side, she was considerably prettier than those who went before. In death likewise, she was unlike the rest, but we will put those issues aside for a moment or two and look briefly at the last night of her young life.

At a quarter to midnight on Thursday November 8th 1888, a rather drunken Kelly was seen by Mary Cox, a fellow prostitute from Miller's Court, in the presence of a stout man with a blotchy face, small whiskers and a carroty coloured moustache. The chap was carrying a pail of beer. Cox exchanges words with Kelly, who breaks into song. "Only a violet from mother's grave", - a popular music hall song at the time, and as the title suggests, is quite a depressing little dirge. Regardless of this fact, Kelly, to the annoyance of residents nearby, howls out the song on and off for over an hour.

Carrotty man and his bucket of liquor may or may not have entered 13 Miller's Court and had sex with Kelly, but at 2 a.m., she had certainly parted company with him, for she is seen by George Hutchinson at Flower and Dean Street. Immediately prior to this sighting, Hutchinson notes a male standing on the corner of Thrawl Street.

Kelly, who obviously knows Hutchinson, asks him for money, but the latter declines, as he has spent what he had "going to Romford." Kelly politely wishes him a good morning and walks off towards Thrawl Street in search of those elusive pennies. It is here that Kelly meets the man whom Hutchinson has passed earlier. A friendly exchange takes place and the two head off in mutual and contractual agreement towards Dorset Street.

Aided by the dull glow of a gas lamp, Hutchinson gives an incredibly detailed description of this man and significantly his attire and adornments. The man, who Hutchinson alleges is carrying that familiar "small package" in his hand, is described thus: He has a pale complexion, a slight moustache turned up at the corners, dark hair, dark eyes, and bushy eyebrows. He is, according to Hutchinson, of "Jewish appearance." The man is wearing a soft felt hat pulled down over his eyes, a long dark coat trimmed in astrakhan, a white collar with a black necktie fixed with a horseshoe pin. He wears dark spats over light button-over boots. A massive gold chain is in his waistcoat with a large seal with a red stone hanging from it. He carries kid gloves in his right hand and a small package in his left. He is 5' 6" or 5' 7" tall and about 35 or 36 years old. Hutchinson follows the pair to the vicinity of Miller's Court, and then waits outside, watching, for forty five minutes.

Our well dressed chap must have been a very brave, (or foolish) man indeed, wandering abroad with such trappings of richness – all begging to be taken from him, particularly in this area of Whitechapel. Is it little wonder that George Hutchinson makes such close scrutiny – or is it? I feel very uncomfortable reading the statement made by Hutchison for a number of reasons.

a) He waits three days before coming forward and offering information to the police. One would have thought that particularly, knowing Kelly, he would have been hammering at the Commercial Street detectives' office as soon as he found out about her murder. Was there a reason for this delay?

b) Why on earth did Hutchinson make such a detailed mental note of the sartorial and decorative state of our Jewish-looking chap? After all, prostitutes were picked up in this area at all times of the day and night. Why is this solicitation so different?

c) Why does he hang around for forty five minutes?

Perhaps my suspicions are raised by the investigation of similar incidents, but if the average time it takes for a prostitute to service her client is 15 – 30 minutes, and if Bejewelled Man has to leave the domicile of Kelly by first entering a dark yard, then maybe, in his post coital state he would make an ideal target for the forcible removal of that gold trinketry hanging from his waistcoat.

George, by his own admission has spent all of his brass on a journey to Romford. With very little effort he could incapacitate Bejewelled Man and realise a few quid by pawning that gold Albert and whatever else he was decorated with that morning.

We may be doing Hutchinson a great disservice, but it strikes me that one with criminal intent; a dishonest man, would be given little credence as a witness by the police. (One of the main investigating officers, Inspector Abberline is understood to have said that he believed Hutchinson was telling the truth, but this does not explain the man's reasons.) Again, just imagine a defence barrister setting about Hutchinson as he stands in the witness box proclaiming his social standing. Something is very wrong with Hutchinson's statement of facts and motives. Something is also very wrong with what came next.

Various statements were made to police by those who claimed to have seen or heard Mary Jane during the next few hours, but these carry little credence if we are to believe the time of death given during a post mortem and crime scene examination of the corpse. (see details below)

We must therefore step ahead to the cold light of day, when John McCarthy, who owned Miller's Court and to whom Mary Jane owed rent, sent his assistant Thomas Bowyer to collect the outstanding debt. The time of that visit was around 10.45 a.m. on 9th November and receiving no response to his repeated knocks, Bowyer pushed aside the curtains in a previously broken window pane, finding a scene of carnage within. Police and medical men were soon on the scene and Dr. Thomas Bond, whom we mentioned earlier in this work, carried out an examination of the corpse.

He stated: "The body was lying naked in the middle of the bed, the shoulders flat but the axis of the body inclined to the left side of the bed. The head was turned on the left cheek. The left arm was close to the body with the forearm flexed at a right angle and lying across the abdomen. The right arm was slightly abducted from the body and rested on the mattress. The elbow was bent, the forearm supine with the fingers clenched. The legs were wide apart, the left thigh at right angles to the trunk and the right forming an obtuse angle with the pubes.

The whole of the surface of the abdomen and thighs was removed and the abdominal cavity emptied of its viscera. The breasts were cut off, the arms mutilated by several jagged wounds and the face hacked beyond recognition of the features. The tissues of the neck were severed all round down to the bone.

The viscera were found in various parts viz: the uterus and kidneys with one breast under the head, the other breast by the right foot, the liver between the feet, the intestines by the right side and the spleen by the left side of the body. The flaps removed from the abdomen and thighs were on a table.

The bed clothing at the right corner was saturated with blood, and on the floor beneath was a pool of blood covering about two feet square. The wall by the right side of the bed and in a line with the neck, was marked by blood which had struck it in a number of separate splashes.

The face was gashed in all directions, the nose, cheeks, eyebrows, and ears being partly removed. The lips were blanched and cut by several incisions running obliquely down to the chin. There were also numerous cuts extending irregularly across all the features.

The neck was cut through the skin and other tissues right down to the vertebrae, the fifth and sixth being deeply notched. The skin cuts in the front of the neck showed distinct ecchymosis. (*the medical term for a subcutaneous discolouration larger than 1 centimeter, or a hematoma, commonly, but erroneously, called a bruise.*)

The air passage was cut at the lower part of the larynx through the cricoid cartilage.

Both breasts were more or less removed by circular incisions, the muscle down to the ribs being attached to the breasts. The intercostals between the fourth, fifth, and sixth ribs were cut through and the contents of the thorax visible through the openings.

The skin and tissues of the abdomen from the costal arch to the pubes were removed in three large flaps. The right thigh was denuded in front to the bone, the flap of skin, including the external organs of generation, and part of the right buttock. The left thigh was stripped of skin fascia, and muscles as far as the knee.

The left calf showed a long gash through skin and tissues to the deep muscles and reaching from the knee to five inches above the ankle. Both arms and forearms had extensive jagged wounds.

The right thumb showed a small superficial incision about one inch long, with extravasation (*leakage of fluid*) of blood in the skin, and there were several abrasions on the back of the hand moreover showing the same condition.

On opening the thorax it was found that the right lung was minimally adherent by old firm adhesions. The lower part of the lung was broken and torn away. The left lung was intact. It was adherent at the apex and there were a few adhesions over the side. In the substances of the lung there were several nodules of consolidation.

The pericardium was open below and the heart absent. In the abdominal cavity there was some partly digested food of fish and potatoes, and similar food was found in the remains of the stomach attached to the intestines."

(The reference to the heart being absent has long been debated. Was it simply not within the body or had it been removed completely?) Dr. Bond did give an opinion that this was the work of the Ripper, but he was basing his theory upon notes and not firsthand experience.

The murder of Mary Jane Kelly was very different to those of the other canonical victims, Nichols, Eddowes and Stride, and many modern investigators and medical professionals raise doubts as to the author of this crime, believing that it was not a Ripper murder. (We should of course balance this with the opposing opinions, particularly when they are made by individuals with medical or legal credibility.) Whilst I am more comfortable with the non-Ripper explanation, it is not the purpose of this work to explore these theories beyond that necessary to consider William Benjamin Belcher's possible culpability.

Whilst my opinions are firmly held, it does seem cruel to consider that of all of the (possible) victims, Mary Jane Kelly is the only one that we can place our suspect in close proximity to over a decent length of time. For as long as she lived at Miller's Court, William Belcher worked just over the road and may well have known the woman. It would help Dianne's case if Kelly were undoubtedly victim number five, but the doubt cast upon her status makes a foggy issue even more unclear.

One thing is for certain though, regardless of Kelly's status, it was at this point in time, the winter of 1888 that 24 year old William Benjamin Belcher upped sticks and removed his brood from 20 Grove Street in favour of colder climes up North. If indeed it was the metaphorical heat that he was running from, then this was a shrewd and very necessary move.

This transition saw not only the inexplicable change of surname, but also a break with everyone and everything that he knew or had known. Even if Belcher had wished to make a clean break of things for *normal* reasons – a new job, new opportunities etc., then it would not have been necessary to do more than relocate and announce his arrival. William Belcher was very definitely running from something – and something big at that.

One more item of note should be mentioned regarding a George Hutchinson. The Sheffield Evening Telegraph, on 15th January 1889, whilst reporting on the murder of John Gill (see later), carries a story titled, "Is he the Whitechapel Murderer?" It mentions the fact that George Hutchinson, on the run from Panama for two or three years following the Ripper-style murder of a respectable woman, may well be Jack himself. Same George? One to research perhaps.

New beginnings, old habits.

The Headland at Hartlepool is a perfect place for a man to disappear. Standing in the shadow of the ancient tower of Saint Hilda's Church listening to the waves crash in along the coast, it must have seemed to William Belcher, or William Williams as he now called himself, that the clatter of London and Whitechapel were a million miles away.

The call of gulls and the endless line of grey-sailed

colliers and merchantmen queuing up along the coast, waiting for favourable tides, bore no resemblance to the filthy city that he had left just a few months earlier. Here among the Georgian quayside dwellings and the huddled twists of cobbled streets young William could breathe again. Whatever demons had forced him from the capital were now long gone. Here he was a free man; free to come and go as he pleased, safe in the knowledge that whatever mysteries he was concealing, whatever hounds were on his trail, no one would ever find him.

Just a few steps from his lodgings William could lean against the promenade rails and look out at the bustle of activity down at Hartlepool. The busy little port and the smoking chimneys offered him work as a boiler cleaner; a second chance, a home and sometime in the future – a long time off in the new century, a place to be buried with the darkness of his soul and the secrets of his past.

To the north, a great curve of coastline swept out as far as the eye could see; the port at Sunderland to its farthest point and the collieries and smoking cokeworks at Seaham sitting above jagged limestone cliffs in the shelter of the great bay. On a good day, scrambling along the coastal paths, a man could walk to Seaham Harbour in just a few hours. That day it seems may have been drawing ever closer.

August 1st 1889 dawned hot and dry. The Headland promenade and the rock pools were full of children and picnicking families. Men were pulling on their boots and taking to the stony paths by the sea. Workmen sweated and old fishermen smoked their clay pipes under the tall gun batteries that guarded the fragile peace. The parks and the flower shows and the Great Regatta up at Seaham were drawing in crowds and summer wrapped itself like a cloying blanket around the coast, its huddle of seaside towns, and of course, William Benjamin Williams. Life – this new life - was sweet indeed.

In a week's time William would celebrate his 25th year. It was time to make merry; and what better way to reward one's self than with the greatest prize of all? The taking of a human life.

2nd August 1889 had seen listless promenaders sweating under crinolines and shawls. Sun scorched children peeled the skin from crimson backs and contemplated their bronzed knees and gritty toes. Tiddlers in rock pools had long been captured and condemned to death in festering jam jars and now, as dusk fell, weary parents dragged their broods away from the beaches and back into the smoky shadows of pits, and the long twisting terraces that climbed away from the Durham coastline. It was in one such terrace at Seaham Harbour, that a young pitman named James Winter sat contemplating all that was wonderful in his own little world. Despite the fact that he was struggling with money problems and ill health following an accident underground, he did have a priceless jewel in the shape of his seven year old daughter, Caroline. The child was his life; she was the one who kept him smiling through the long days, she was his future - the one who would tend to his needs in old age; and right at that moment she was also something else – she was very hungry.

James took a ha'penny from the mantelpiece and threw it over to Caroline, asking her to run to Mrs. Donaldson's corner shop to buy two eggs. The bairn, as north east folk call children, took the money and scampered a hundred yards or so to the shop, where she met ten year old Ann Cowell. It was here, shortly before 9 p.m. that the two were approached by a man who took hold of Caroline's arm and told her that he was her cousin. "I'll give you half a shilling," he told her, "If you come with me."

Whoever this man was he was extremely self confident and had no problem with being seen on the streets as he selected and lured away his victim. According to Ann, who noted the man's trampish appearance, battered old hat and brown moustache, it looked as if the two were known to each other and Caroline joked with the shabby stranger who now offered her a ha'penny instead of the promised sixpence. Caroline and the man went into the shop and "bought some bullets", (North East slang for sweets) including coconut nibs which were popular at the time. And then he led her away towards Sebastopol Terrace and the gate that led down the steep steps to the rock pools and Seaham Harbour bathing sands. Hand in hand, with Ann Cowell watching on in trepidation, the two disappeared into the night.

When his little jewel did not come home, James Winter began to fret, calling upon all and sundry to help him look for her. Their searches were fruitless and by dawn on 3rd August it seemed as though the child had disappeared into thin air. The only suspicious activity to be uncovered by the police was a sighting of a man described as similar to Caroline's abductor, heading off along the cliffs towards Hartlepool.

As the early morning sea fret lifted from the Harbour, two young brothers, John and David Hamilton were walking on the beach near to Featherbed Rocks when they saw a little bundle lying in a rock pool. Curious as to what treasures they may have stumbled upon the pair scrambled over to take a closer look.

Caroline Winter's young body lay smashed below the cliffs. Her skull had been caved in and her brains were exposed to the air. Her face showed signs of mutilation and her tiny arm lay covering the savagery inflicted upon her. As well as having been "violated in the most terrible way", the child had also suffered the most awful damage to her abdomen. Such was the ferocity of the attack and the resultant injuries that the local newspapers, so often the first to revel in the spectacle of murder, wrote the story and described her injuries in the most circumspect and restrained of ways.

The Sunderland Echo on 5th August 1889, reported:

"She was lying on her back with one of her tiny arms lying across her bruised and disfigured face. Her arm was marked and her hand and fingers lacerated and bleeding. The base of her skull and the top of her forehead were beaten in to a fearful extent. A portion of the brain was protruding. The throat of the deceased was marked as though severe pressure with fingers had been made; whilst the lower part of her body presented an appearance too ghastly to be contemplated."

Once news reached the public, thousands were arriving on trains to visit the murder site (pictured below). Enterprising locals set up cameras to take tourist photographs on Featherbed Rocks; some gathered water in little bottles from the bloodied rock pools and "scarcely a soul left without taking a pebble or a piece of rock as a souvenir of the murder".

Within days of the discovery, men, particularly those of an itinerant nature, were being arrested and dragged to the police station at Seaham. (The practice of indiscriminately arresting every known local criminal or individuals of a similar appearance to the culprit, more in hope that someone may just crack and provide information, continued well into the twentieth century. Rarely was there any substantiation for these arrests other than to appease the public.) One unfortunate and very innocent man was questioned and subsequently released without charge, walking into a huge crowd of bloodthirsty locals who were waiting outside. It is no surprise that his broken body was found next morning in the same spot as that where young Caroline Winter had perished. Rumours abounded that he was indeed the culprit and in a fit of remorse had thrown himself over the cliffs in a final act of self punishment. Without doubt he had been punished, but this was no suicide. It was murder.

And so, as William Williams celebrated with a pint or two on the eve of his birthday, a few miles away James Winter followed the cortege that took his tiny daughter's body from Little John Street and off to be buried at the

Parish Church. Thousands of locals, dressed in black or sporting bands upon their sleeves lined the route and shared his pain, but none could take away the terrible grief that he felt at losing his precious little jewel.

James Winter would die of a broken heart in just a few short months, but that would mean nothing to he who carried out the rape and murder of his baby. After all, what was one more death to a man for whom death was simply a necessary by-product of sick sexual pleasure. Caroline Winter's murder would never be avenged. James Winter's death was simply collateral damage.

Back in 1889, there was speculation about the author of this crime and whether it may have been Jack the Ripper's work. After the death of Mary Jane Kelly, political pressure on the police hierarchy from Parliament and indeed the Queen herself, was such that it was far easier to sever any remote connection rather than admit the possibility that our man had evaded capture yet again. The authorities simply wanted the Ripper out of their hair. Subsequent prostitute murders in London, many perpetrated with extreme ferocity, would be moved into the "quite acceptable" basket, and there they would remain. As far as the boys in blue were concerned, Jack was dead and buried.

Friday nights down south must have seemed to the police a lot quieter now that their man had gone. The fact remains that 2nd August, the day that Caroline Edith Winter met her own Ripper, was also a Friday. Just another coincidence? Was it another coincidence that on the Friday night prior to the murder of Caroline, just north of Hartlepool, two other girls had been indecently assaulted and an attempt made to abduct them by a man with the exact same appearance as Caroline's murderer? If so, it was not the first coincidence in Dianne's story and it certainly would not be the last.

I will kill a child next time.

At the time of the Ripper enquiry there were a number of peripheral murders, including those of children, which were associated with the main investigation, so that of Caroline Winter does not stand alone.

The police at the time of the Whitechapel murders were, it is estimated, handling around 1000 letters a week, all of which had to be read, and all of which offered help, advice, nominations and of course, confessions in varying degrees of lunacy. The press and indeed other organisations also suffered from a deluge of such written communications. The most interesting survive to this day.

Among the helpful advice were suggestions that hand bells should be left on every pavement, thus allowing an attacked prostitute to reach out, grab the instrument and ring frantically for a constable while her innards were being reassembled. Others suggested leaving spring loaded dummy prostitutes attractively posed on the streets, with open legs and arms, inviting the Ripper to engage in intimacy and thereby activating the spring which would lock immovably around his waist, trapping him in terrible coitus interruptus until the arrival of the boys in blue.

Others, signed Jack, sent shivers down the spine of those who read them. They taunted and bragged and gave uncanny predictions, some of which bore close resemblance to the truth, whether past or future. Like the murders, the letters remain contentious and surround themselves in suspicion and speculation. One of them, at first seemingly innocuous in the matter of R. v William Benjamin Belcher, would once again provide Dianne with food for thought. As usual, the fare was bitter tasting and would have been far better if left lying on the plate.

On 26th November, the author of a *Ripper* letter claimed that he would take the lives of some young lads – "like the printing lads in the city". This time, he said, chillingly, that he would do a better job than he had hitherto performed on the women – he would take out their hearts, he warned. That prediction would soon come true.

On the morning of Thursday, 29th December 1888, 8 year old John Gill told his mother that he was to spend a few hours helping milk carrier William Barrett delivering supplies around the Manningham area of Bradford. This was normal practice for the lad, who would return home for breakfast after the round had finished.

The pair were seen together by various witnesses, but it seems that the lad, unusually, left his toils after the penultimate delivery in order to take his morning meal. He did not return home. Police were alerted and during the next two days, their efforts to find the lad proved fruitless. Barrett remained attentive during that time, giving information to Mr. And Mrs. Gill, as well as calling at their home on the Friday to enquire after the lad.

At half past seven on New Year's Eve, a butcher's lad named Joseph Bucke (or Buckle) visited the stable of his master in order to attend to a horse there. The premises lay close to the route taken by William Barrett on his rounds. Bucke noticed a heap lying next to the coach-house, and being dark, he procured a light in order to investigate the object further. He had discovered the body of John Gill.

Gill's naked corpse, which was wrapped in his own coat, was horribly mutilated, his legs having been cut off and laid beside the body. Two stab wounds were inflicted to the child's chest. The body had been ripped open and the heart was pulled out and thrust under the chin. Other organs had also been removed along with part of the lad's ears. John's boots had been placed inside of his body cavity, and other mutilations that the Victorian press thought too sensitive to detail had also been carried out. We must assume that these involved his genitals.

Around the lad's neck was a scrap of shirting. It is interesting to note that this detail is of relevance to the Whitechapel murders too. The Ripper did not remove the women's scarves and it has been suggested that partial strangulation in order to reduce blood pressure may have been part of the killer's M.O.

The clothes which were beside the body showed no obvious damage or contamination, so they had obviously been removed prior to the butchery. The scene likewise showed no traces of blood, indicating to attending doctors that the murder had taken place elsewhere and the corpse had been spirited to its present location. 23 year old William Barrett, the obvious suspect, found himself languishing in police custody before the day was out.

It was reported to police that at 10 a.m. on the day that the lad went missing, a local man, Mr. Cahill returned home after being away for the night with his wife, to find that his house had been feloniously entered. Furniture had been strewn about and placed beside crossed knives on a kitchen table was a card announcing that Jack the Ripper had been.

The Sheffield Evening Telegraph reported on the first of January 1889, that the "calling card" of which many were available in the area, contained a printed joke on one side while the Ripper legend had been pencilled on the other. While Cahill does not seem to have corroborated the assertion that the incident was a hoax, perpetrated by a female member of the family, the story was nevertheless carried and repeated here and elsewhere.

In the same publication, beneath the calling card paragraph, it is reported that "the police have confessed that they have found insanity in the prisoner (Barrett's) family." Chillingly and as a strange aside, they conclude in the article, "the missing lung has been found inside of the stomach."

While newspaper-led anti Barrett feelings were at boiling point in Bradford, the man himself remained calm and rigorously maintained his innocence. Statements against him were mounting however, including one from a Salvationist named John Thomas Dyer and another from a cook, Fanny Turrell both of which stated he had been seen carrying a parcel away from his stable at the time of Gill's disappearance. Dyer's sanity was brought into question, particularly as one doctor who was refused permission to testify, claimed that despite colleagues' findings that he (Dyer) was fit to give evidence, the opposite was very much true.

And so, blood stained material, knives that had been used for other than cutting bread and a whole host of police evidence was later produced and then disintegrated into dust. On 12th January 1889, at Leeds, the bill against Barrett was refused due to the "wholly circumstantial nature of the evidence". His clothes and property were returned and he walked away from court a free man. Until 5th February that is, when he was rearrested by the police on a coroner's warrant and once more appeared in the dock.

On 11th March 1889, at Leeds Winter Assizes, the fiasco continued when the prosecution finally admitted defeat and offered no evidence against William Barrett. He was once more released from custody and this time remained a free man.

On Saturday 23rd March, riding upon horseback and accompanied by dozens of carts, gigs and other decorated vehicles, over 1000 people turned out to celebrate Barrett's homecoming at Manningham. Tea was provided for participants and over £500 was raised to pay for his defence. Rain stopped play that afternoon, but the popular feeling had already been demonstrated, that Barrett had certainly not murdered John Gill. If not he, then who had carried out this act of barbarism?

It may or may not be relevant, but looking back at the Ripper's alleged prediction that he would visit the country and kill a child, it is worthy of note that William Benjamin Belcher and the Barretts here mentioned, milk carriers all, are related by marriage. William Barrett's father, Metropolitan constable Frederick Barrett married Elizabeth Thoms whose brother Alfred was a Whitechapel dairyman. The Belchers, one time neighbours of the Barretts and Thoms, married into the family. It is not beyond the imagination to suppose that *visits to the country* may have been a reference to Bradford – and relations thereat.

In a postscript to the affair, which remains an open and unsolved case, a report appeared in local newspapers a year after Gill's murder, stating that the culprits were a group of boys. The informant, who could not "live with his guilt", had confessed to a local vicar. The story however would become chip paper in a very short time.

More Ripper letters would be received by the Metropolitan Police, commemorating the Bradford murder. "I riped (sic) up a little boy in Bradford," the author gloats. On 16th January he makes another reference to the Bradford trip. While the John Gill murder is an aside when it comes to the subject of Jack the Ripper, it is for Dianne, an aside with yet another Belcher coincidence written into it. And if that were not enough, her genealogical journey would turn up yet another anomaly – and perhaps the strangest yet.

Dear Diary

When, in 1992, a gentleman named Michael Barrett handed a document purporting to be the diary of Jack the Ripper to author Shirley Harrison, there began a saga to rival the best and worst of TV soaps. The diary, inferred to have been written by James Maybrick, was allegedly discovered in Liverpool and handed to Barrett for his onward transmission and personal benefit. Michael Barrett would subsequently launch into solicitor-witnessed denials and all manner of contemporary side-issues, all of which added to the shabby hoax versus Maybrick-was-the-Ripper debate that continues unabated.

Over the years, present diary owner Robert Smith and Ms. Harrison, aided and abetted by learned professionals and scientists from both sides of the Atlantic, would endeavour to prove beyond reasonable doubt that the diary was written by the Ripper himself, over a century ago. These studies, together with assertions and opinions offered by others who were watching on the sidelines, produced so many conflicting opinions that the whole issue became incredibly diluted and difficult to follow. Nevertheless, there is still a dedicated team of supporters who firmly believe that the fabric of the diary is contemporary with the Whitechapel murders and was indeed written by Maybrick.

One time scrap dealer Michael Barrett, initially alleged that the diary was given to him by a chap called Tony Devereaux, in a pub. I am not sure why the pub suffix was important enough to mention, but that story would later be changed when up stepped Barrett's wife Ann (nee Graham) with "the truth". She claimed that it had actually been in her family for as long as she could remember, and that the transaction twixt her husband and Devereaux was designed to prevent conflict with her father.

The whole issue as you will see, even at this early stage becomes very messy. But, regardless of the mess, the present owner of the diary, Robert Smith – a very well connected London Publishing Agent, together with author Shirley Harrison, having invested much in its investigation, are more than happy with its origins and authenticity. Ms. Harrison's book on the subject rises above the snapping wolves of doubt and presents a very well written and convincing argument. Indeed, Mr. Maybrick and his complex and philandering lifestyle deservedly place him in a line-up of likely characters.

But, before we stray too far from the original question of William Belcher / Williams and his association with yet another aspect of the Ripper juggernaut, Dianne Bainbridge told me that the diaries had originated not from Liverpool, but Hartlepool. And not just Hartlepool, but the Headland, which, tagged on to the north of its bigger neighbour, is really no more than a village in size and population.

When I spoke to Mr. Smith about William Belcher and the work that we were engaged in, mentioning Dianne's statement about the North East connection, he told me quite flatly that there was no link at all. I thanked him for an enjoyable and informative discussion and thereafter suggested to Dianne that she rethink her Hartlepool Headland connection. I should have known better. Out came a well researched family tree:

Ann Graham, who claimed that the diary was in the family vaults for "as long as she could remember", was born in Liverpool in 1950. Her father William was born in Hartlepool. Her grandfather William, likewise was a

Hartlepool lad, born in 1884. His first wife was named Rebecca Jones. His second was Scouser Edith Formby. It is she who is alleged to have been associated with Maybrick.

There is another generation of Hartlepool Grahams, that being Anne's great grandfather Adam (1847-98). Thus there is indeed a Headland link, but if that is not coincidence enough, then we must look to William (then Williams) as he settles into the new century and his little terraced house in the shadow of Saint Hilda's Church. The Graham family were, according to the census records, his next door neighbours.

Of course, this association proves little other than the fact that yet another coincidence had reared up from the pages of census and registers long past, linking William Benjamin Belcher with Whitechapel and its four months of hell. That events in 1992 Liverpool and 1888 Whitechapel can be linked to within the thickness of a brick wall to the Belchers takes some believing, and makes Dianne's story as confusing as it is compelling.

The problem with confessions.

The murder of Jane Beadmore, or Jane Savage as she was often called, back in September of 1888 caused a ripple of unease not only in Victorian London, but also on the pages of Patricia Cornwell's book, *Portrait of a Killer*. If ever there was an example of appalling misinformation coupled with an attempt to take a man who was documented as being abroad and bring him all the way back to Gateshead – which place he had probably never heard of – for the purpose of attaching guilt to his wholly innocent bones – then this is it.

28 year old Jane Beadmore was found dead on Birtley Fell, near Gateshead, an area that is well known to me, and which over a century ago was little more than a scattering of farms, pitmen's cottages and the ancillary buildings that supported many similar north east mining communities. Despite Ms Cornwell's assertions that Jane "was rumoured to have" low moral values, there is absolutely no evidence at all to corroborate this fabricated allegation and it has to be accepted that the victim was a perfectly normal young woman without convictions or blemishes on her character.

Because the girl's injuries bore similarities with those of the Whitechapel victims, local detectives contacted the Metropolitan Police, who duly facilitated the attendance of Dr. George Bagster Philips and Detective Inspector Roots, both of whom had knowledge of the Ripper's recent modus operandi. After being met by the Chief Constable and Superintendent Harrison, they examined the murder scene and thereafter the corpse, which reposed in nearby White House Cottage. Unsurprisingly, they quickly decided that the victim and he who had brought about her demise were not connected with the London enquiry; they lunched and ignoring the huge throng of reporters who had gathered waiting for a verdict, headed back home on the first available train.

Dr. Bagster Philips was reportedly an incredibly focussed individual, sometimes so much so that he would ignore peripheral evidence, such as the bloodied neckerchief belonging to Annie Chapman, presented to him, acknowledged and immediately forgotten. On occasions his assumptions and professional opinions were quite incorrect, and thus he may at times have pointed police enquiries in the wrong direction. Regardless of these minor irritations his professional abilities and dedication were held in the highest esteem by his employers.

Local detectives had no doubt been praying that the Metropolitan Police would take the case from their hands, saving them from the crippling financial burden of a murder enquiry and the subsequent manhunt that would place them and their efforts under the scrutiny of every breakfasting newspaper reader in the country. It was now back to the drawing board and the old and well-trusted maxim that three quarters of all murders are committed by the one you love...and he who was closest to the heart of Jane Beadmore was 22 year old William Waddell.

Waddell was well known in the area for his strange habits, including the propensity to disappear into the country when the mood overtook him. The Sunderland Echo, on 5th October, after Waddell's capture reported that "a suspicion very generally prevails that the prisoner's mind is affected and this is strengthened by the moroseness of his manner ordinarily and by the fact that he has on more than one occasion mysteriously disappeared from Birtley."

So, after local busybodies reported that he had been seen jumping down pit shafts and sharpening knives on stones, Waddell was in fact doing what he was known to do – mysteriously disappearing. His subsequent travels took him through Northumberland and up to Berwick, each mile sapping his energy, mental stamina and strength, before he was finally apprehended by a wool merchant in Kirk Yetholm.

When, thoroughly exhausted and too weary to protest, he was handed over to the village bobby, Police Constable Thompson, Waddell is alleged to have made a confession which was written in the officer's notebook. When asked to produce this in court, Thompson produced a pocket book with the relevant pages torn out. He explained that the sheets were burned because they contained sensitive material on the other side. That the judge accepted this statement beggars belief. That Thompson got away with it astounds me. The pair should have been flogged. Had I ever pulled the same stunt in a modern day court of law, I would expect to be sent down for destruction of material evidence and perverting the course of justice. Thompson got a pat on the back for his heroism and made a few quid out of the public purse for his attendance at court.

Once he had been returned to Gateshead following his arrest, Waddell remained in cells there for some time. That he was well known to be at a mental disadvantage seemed to make little difference to his accusers, but despite their best efforts Waddell never clearly confessed. He did comment, in an unofficial conversation with a constable – a cell block conversation - that he would never do such a thing had he been in his right mind. That is not a confession, nor is telling the police that he was so drunk that he lost his senses.

These days a person with learning difficulties or who is suspected to be less than fully functioning mentally would have the services of an appropriate adult, or indeed a medical specialist and he would never be told repeatedly that he was a guilty man. Tell someone like Waddell that he is a murderer enough times and he will eventually believe you. Someone who craves attention will tell you whatever he thinks will please you. Such is the fuel for false confessions the world over.

And yes, Waddell is supposed to have confessed at the last minute to some visiting holy man, but this is hardly the same as being proved beyond reasonable doubt – not on wholly circumstantial evidence, to have committed the crime. Imagine the privations that the man had endured and the state of his mind at the last – hours before his life was going to be taken from him.

William Waddell may well have been the killer. William Waddell may have indeed, after reading reports about the Whitechapel murders, sliced open his girlfriend after some stupid row or in a fit of blind jealousy, but the process of law and the appallingly unethical presentation and disappearance (or fabrication) of critical evidence should have ended this case long before its conclusion. Durham County Constabulary wanted a guilty verdict and they got it.

The point of the matter is very simple. As with the tramp whose demise at Seaham Harbour ended a search for Caroline Winter's true killer, William Waddell's conviction and execution was a total shambles. It is only when we can be confident that the trial and subsequent finding of guilt were healthy and ethical that we can tick the box and eliminate the Whitechapel Ripper from this or any other murder.

The transition from Belcher to Williams

If indeed the Belcher clan packed up their few belongings and at the end of 1888 hurried northwards to escape in Hartlepool, then Annie Belcher would have been pregnant with a son who would later bear the name of his proud father. Willie Belcher was born on 26th June 1889, just a few weeks before the murder of Caroline Winter. He would be registered by Annie on the same day that Caroline's relatives were preparing for her funeral a few miles up the coast. Willie would be registered in the name of Belcher, like his sibling James William who was born in the January of 1892. But there the name of Belcher dies.

In fact, the name seems to have died as far as the official census is concerned, the previous year, as the family are shown to be in residence at Grace Street, Hartlepool, but now under the name of Williams. Subsequent official records will adopt Williams as a surname and Belcher will become a thing of the past.

The 1891 census back at Grove Street will show Benjamin, William's father, back in residence, together with the three youngest children.

The new Williams clan will remain in the town of Hartlepool for years to come, later generations being blissfully unaware of their antecedent history. Perhaps it is just as well.

Closing boxes

I would like to have told Dianne Bainbridge right at the beginning to put away her little box of family conundrums; to pack up her folders of Ancestry prints, family trees and copious notes. I would like to have told her that William Benjamin Belcher had a very simple reason for changing his name and heading off to the north east of England to begin his new life. The fact is, I couldn't – and at no time during our association have I been able to find justification for directing her journey toward the buffers.

Her story is a series of extraordinary coincidences and simple facts that raise far-from-simple questions and explanations. The more one digs the more confusing and tantalising the story becomes. As with some of the other, credible Ripper suspects, there has to be a jury of open minds in order to stand our man against the wall and tarnish what may in reality be an unblemished personality and antecedent history of impeccable standards. I believe that any jury of twelve good and honest individuals would have been swayed by the avalanche of coincidences – all circumstantial, that it would fall upon them to consider.

Would they find William Benjamin Belcher guilty? I think that they, like many juries I have known over the years, would have reluctantly allowed the defendant to walk free, but that discharge would have been accompanied by a nagging tug of unease; that the man had pulled the wool over their eyes or would be slicing open someone else's throat within the week.

When Dianne asks what possible conclusions can be drawn from the story and the evidence that she has thus far produced (there is much more that she needs to clarify and research – facts that the archives seem reluctant as yet to divulge) I have to tell her that the answer to her question is as complex as the question itself.

Did Belcher kill five women in Whitechapel? That question brings with it the additional problem of Mary Kelly and modern thinking about her inclusion in the canonical list. To accept that Belcher had what it takes to become a serial killer we must consider the recently discovered criterion: that he was a psychopath possessed of the Warrior Gene (MAOA-L gene variant) and that he suffered some form of abuse as a child. We have no way of knowing this of course but we can point towards there being the next critical element, a pre crime stressor event. With the majority of modern serial killers such a critical event is apparent, and in Belcher's case, the traumatic demise of his mother and the resultant effect that it had upon him could not fail to have a significant impact in later life. With this in mind, he may well have been an ideal candidate for a future career as a killer.

That he had cause to hate prostitutes and prostitution we can also accept on not just one, but two counts. His mother's possible prostitution during the last years of her tragic life, and the Esther Belcher affair that so rocked late 19th century England.

He has access to the streets in the early hours and is in proven close proximity to Kelly. (Consider again the possible need to separate Kelly from the rest.) Regarding the other victims we have geographical access and the ability to read and predict the activities of the police beat officers – so necessary to avoid capture when working within such a tight time frame for murder.

We have local knowledge and residence well within the accepted seven mile circle attributed to serial killers and their primary offences - a rule that we should considerably shorten in view of the parochial nature of Victorian criminals compared with modern car-borne killers. There is also knowledge of butchery and anatomy and a family whose antecedents are certainly dodgy with a leaning towards knife crime and violence.

The geographic link to, and the nature of the killing of little Caroline Winter in 1889 is uncanny and worth, even if the police disregarded his involvement in the London killings, an arrest on suspicion of this offence.

Even the Bradford slaying is worthy of consideration based upon the family links – the society of milk carriers certainly extended far beyond Whitechapel.

All in all, I cannot put Dianne's mind at rest and nor can I suggest that she aborts the quest to untarnish her man. (Don't forget that the object of her endeavours was always to place a distance between Belcher and murder, not the other way around.) If ever a scrap of paper created a monster, then the memento mori of little James Webber is a candidate for mischief of the highest order.

Seven months down the line and with the jury still out on William Benjamin Belcher / Williams, we have to accept the fact that we may never know if he was complicit in murder, but then again, he fares no differently to any and every other suspect put forward in print or film over the years. Our man, along with his contemporaries simply took his secrets with him.

If Dianne's journey started with a small coffin and a corpse that has long rotted and turned to dust then so must this stage of her journey. Standing by William William's grave on a hot August day, coincidentally the 125th anniversary of Martha Tabram's murder, it is easy to forget that the man who sleeps beneath our feet may have belonged to a time and a place that lies far beyond the boundaries of our imagination. We will never know if his sleep has been as untroubled as the peaceful surroundings into which he was interred, or if those who gathered around his grave on 21st March 1936 knew of the secrets that he took there with him.

William Williams left behind a family who mourned him and a legacy that would lie untouched for almost a century. He left behind a trail of clues and coincidences that would serve to deepen and not clarify the conundrum. He achieved in death that which he had sought in his 24th year and beyond – anonymity. He was simply the grey man who disappeared, losing his identity and slipping into the safety of obscurity.

One wonders why he hung on so tightly to that tiny scrap of paper – that memento mori - the only souvenir from the year of Jack the Ripper's reign and his own transformation from William Belcher to William Williams; the only clue that Dianne Bainbridge needed to uncover that which he hoped to forget – his past.

Perhaps the little treasure and its meaning were deliberately left; a final taunt, a final sneer at the world that he deceived for so long. Memento Mori simply means, remember that you will die. What better words could a murderer leave behind? What better words to whisper in the ear of your victim as you take a knife to her throat?

Remember that you will die.

Appendix one: *Map of Whitechapel (Casebook.org)*

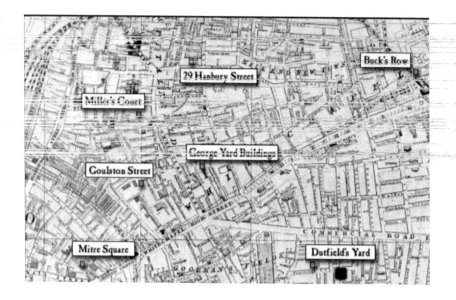

Appendix Two: Webber and Belcher Family Trees:

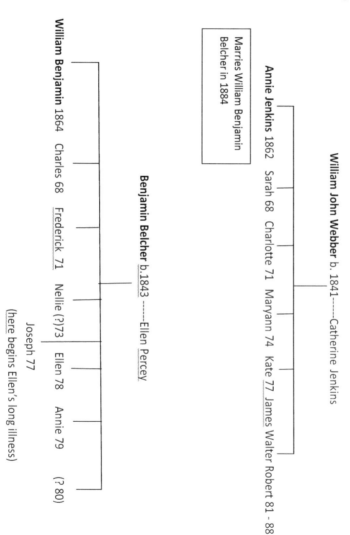

William John Webber b. 1841-----Catherine Jenkins

Marries William Benjamin Belcher in 1884

Annie Jenkins 1862   Sarah 68   Charlotte 71   Maryann 74   Kate 77   James Walter Robert 81 - 88

Benjamin Belcher b. 1843 -----Ellen Percey

William Benjamin 1864   Charles 68   Frederick 71   Nellie (?)73   Ellen 78   Annie 79   (? 80)

Joseph 77
(here begins Ellen's long illness)

155

Appendix Three: William Benjamin Belcher / Williams family tree.

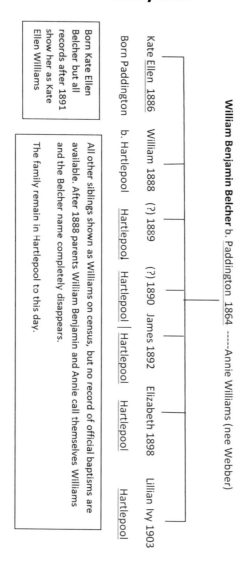

William Benjamin Belcher b. Paddington 1864 ------Annie Williams (nee Webber)

Kate Ellen 1886   William 1888   (?) 1889   (?) 1890   James 1892   Elizabeth 1898   Lillian Ivy 1903

Born Paddington   b. Hartlepool   Hartlepool   Hartlepool   Hartlepool   Hartlepool   Hartlepool

Born Kate Ellen Belcher but all records after 1891 show her as Kate Ellen Williams

All other siblings shown as Williams on census, but no record of official baptisms are available. After 1888 parents William Benjamin and Annie call themselves Williams and the Belcher name completely disappears.

The family remain in Hartlepool to this day.

Appendix Four: Timeline.

1864: William Benjamin Belcher born in London. The family are well settled. Father Benjamin working as a decorator. Two siblings, Charles and Frederick are born within four years.

1870s: Family fall on hard times. Benjamin has periods of absence and is arrested for drunkenness. Moving into Grove Street, Lisson Grove, they live in the unfurnished basement kitchen.

1875-80. Mother Ellen has a child each year while father absent.

1880: Ellen dies of tuberculosis and sixteen year old William supports the family as a milk carrier. Ellen's death certificate shows that she has had TB for five years and dies through blood loss. She was six months pregnant. Ellen's sister Margaret (spinster housekeeper) is present at the death.

1881: Census shows William still resident at Grove Street. Father Benjamin included on census but pencilled out. Margaret is shown as being wife and mother, although this is incorrect. A lodger has moved in with the family.

1884: William marries Annie Webber. Margaret is a witness. Annie joins the family at Grove Street.

1885: Margaret dies. Benjamin present at death.

1886: Kate Ellen is born to William and Annie.

1888: Annie is present at the death of her young brother, as shown on the memento mori card.

Family move to Hartlepool Headland where William takes on labouring jobs. Sons Willie (89) and James (92) are born and registered as Belcher. By the 1891 census the family have moved a mile further inland and the surname Williams is adopted. Belcher does not appear to have been used again.

1911: Census shows the Williams family still at Hartlepool and two of their children have died. No further birth or death certificates can be traced.

1911 to present: Williams family resident in Hartlepool area.

A note on forensic reconstruction

My work in forensic reconstruction falls within two main categories:

a) The identification of living suspects whose composite likenesses are taken from descriptions provided from victims and witnesses, and

b) The reconstruction, for identification purposes, of  deceased individuals, this process normally being carried out in a mortuary, or from photographs provided by Scenes of Crime Officers.

An example of the former is shown left: The sketch was taken from a victim of rape who, despite what she had suffered, showed remarkable strength and determination in providing me with a detailed description of her city centre attacker. The sketch was shown to officers who were working the relevant beat, and the night following the offence, two female police officers saw a male (right) matching the description near to the original crime scene. Upon the officer's approach, the suspect ran off but was apprehended nearby.

He was subsequently convicted of the rape and received a lengthy term of imprisonment.

While the sketch is not an identical likeness of the suspect, it is what police class as a *type likeness*. Descriptions given by the numerous witnesses in the Whitechapel Enquiry were recorded as written statements and would have been read to officers as they paraded for duty, prior to embarking on their beat duties.

Police at that time rarely used artists, unlike the press, who delighted in the graphic illustration of crime scenes, suspects and particularly the discovery of murdered women. Naked corpses, like the Pinchin Street victim whose torso was discovered on 12th September 1889, provided rare opportunities to show uncovered breasts, which probably boosted newspaper sales significantly. Illustrations of convicted murderers often showed a demonised version of the individual, as in the case of serial killer Mary Ann Cotton, whose true, delicate features were graphically transformed into those of a hardened criminal for public consumption.

Had the Metropolitan or City of London detectives employed a forensic artist, then I believe the overwhelming weight of evidence gleaned from the witnesses would lean towards the Ripper having an *ordinary* or *average* appearance. (Ordinary and average are two terms used over and over again by witnesses who fail to find abnormalities or strong features in a

160

suspect.) Perhaps, as no witness describes overt or unusual features, Jack's image would closer resemble that above, rather than the top-hatted and caped monster whose bogey-man features we seem to mentally conjure when Jack the Ripper's name is mentioned. This is of course entirely due to the demonization process, started by contemporary newspaper editors, and absorbed into popular culture and belief to this day.

The victims of the Whitechapel murders, or more particularly their mortuary photographs, have sadly become iconic in their own right. Books on the subject always seem to show the mortuary photographs, or in Mary Kelly's case, the crime scene photographs, thereby associating a name not to a living individual, but to a corpse.

It has always been a consideration when I have carried out mortuary reconstruction work that the individual who lay before me was someone's son or daughter; was once loved and capable of laughter, despite the hardships and deprivation endured during darker periods of life.

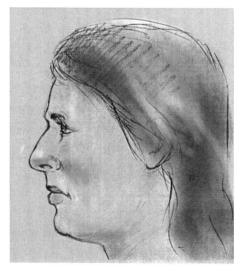

The image shown right was one of a series of mortuary reconstruction sketches taken from the body of a victim whose remains were washed up on a beach at South Shields. Identification was a major issue, as enquiries needed to be undertaken to establish not only who she was but how she had died and by whose hand – if not her own.

We are far too sensitive in this country to publish the photograph of a dead person regardless of how urgently we need to establish facts, and therefore the services of a forensic artist are used.

When local enquiries, using my drawings, failed to put a name to the young lady, national TV appeals eventually succeeded and she was identified as a suicide victim from Eastern Scotland. Thus, after travelling hundreds of miles in the North Sea she was reunited with her grieving family and given a decent burial.

It goes without saying that the longer a victim has been dead, the more difficult it becomes to create a *living likeness* of him or her. Even an individual who has been dead a matter of hours can show a marked change to their normal, living features.

The photographic images of Polly Nichols, Annie Chapman, Liz Stride and Catherine Eddowes were taken after their respective post mortems, and a reconstruction artist would need to bear in mind that the girls had been dead for a good few days, adjustments needing to be considered and incorporated into the final work. The quality of the end product depends upon time spent at the mortuary with the victim, or upon the availability of detailed photographs taken of the deceased.

Mary Kelly, although her crime scene photographs were taken much nearer to her time of death, is of course so badly mutilated that any forensic reconstruction without an X Ray of her skull would be nothing other than a flight of fantasy.

The authors would like to thank:

Jenni Day, Talent TV South, for photographic images and support throughout.

Detective Chief Superintendent Bob Jackson (Retired). For time spent reviewing the manuscript and his valued advice and suggestions.

Dr. B.R. Shepherd for discussions on the medical aspects of the enquiry.

Linda King for proof reading.

Staff at Hartlepool Local Studies for their kindness and assistance.

Mike Covell for photographic contributions and comments based upon his encyclopaedic knowledge of the Ripper enquiry.

Debra Arif, for supplying information that corrected the geographical location and residence of the Belcher family.

The administrators of Casebook.Org website for providing for public consumption a remarkable archive relating to the Whitechapel murders.